1

BUT GOD

HOW HE REWROTE THE LIFE I NEARLY DESTROYED

A Soul ReBirth Story

Written By: Brent Stewart

This is a non-fiction work. All stories are true and drawn from the author's lived experience. Names and details may have been changed to protect privacy where appropriate.

Cover and interior design by Soul Rebirth Designs.

Printed in the United States of America.

First Edition – 2025

For inquiries, speaking engagements, or coaching requests:

soulrebirthdesigns@gmail.com
TikTok / Instagram / Pinterest: @SoulReBirthDesigns
Etsy.com/shop/Soulrebirthdesigns

ISBN: 9798280449923

Dedication

To my son—
You gave me a reason to come home.
Your forgiveness is a gift I'll never stop unwrapping.
Thank you for still believing in me, even when I barely believed in myself.

To my grandson—
You are the new beginning in a story that almost did not make it.
This book is proof that the cycle ends here, and legacy begins now.

To my mom—
Your love carried me through more than I ever had the words to say.
Even when things were messy, your love was steady.
Thank you for being the heartbeat in the background of my story.

To my sister—
You have been my strength, my anchor, and my reminder that real family holds on—even when life falls apart.
Without you, I would have never found my way back.

To my nephews—
To the ones still here: your lives inspire me to stay the course.
And to the ones I have lost you are the ache and the fire in my heart.
Your memory is woven into every page of this story. I carry you with me—always.

And to the man I used to be—
You survived the storm.
You endured the shame.
And you held on just long enough to become someone new.
I honor your pain, because it birthed my purpose.

About This Book

This is not just another recovery story.

This is the raw, unfiltered journey of a man who should have died… but didn't.

A man who lost everything—and then found grace in the rubble.

In these pages, you will walk through addiction, broken promises, family scars, painful truths, relapses, jail cells, and late-night cries to God.

But you will also see redemption unfold—chapter by chapter.

You will see what happens when Jesus meets a man at his lowest… and lifts him higher than he ever imagined possible.

This is not a self-help book.
It is a God-helped-me book.

A story of faith over fear. Grace over guilt. Purpose over pain.

Whether you are in the fight of your life or loving someone who is— this book is for you.

Come as you are.

Leave with hope.

And never forget—God still writes comeback stories.

Table of Contents

Foreword

I first met Brent Stewart on the day he walked through the doors of Teen Challenge of Arizona's Tucson Men's Center. I remember meeting a man who was broken, unsure of who he was or where he was going, yet desperate for something different—something real. As the director of this program, I have had the privilege of watching hundreds of men check in each year. And every so often, someone stands out. There is a look in their eyes—a readiness, a surrender. Brent was one of those men.

What you will read in these pages is more than just a story. It is a testament to God's power to redeem what others may call hopeless. Brent's journey is proof that no one is too far gone, and that no matter how deep the pit, God's grace can reach deeper. It's also a story of grit and surrender—of a man who chose to lay down his old life and step into the one God had always intended for him.

The Brent I know today is not the same man I met that first day. I've witnessed his transformation firsthand—from a life shackled by addiction and sin to one marked by purpose, healing, and the freedom found only in Christ.

His journey has come full circle. So much so, that Brent now serves on our staff at Teen Challenge in Tucson, pouring into the lives of men who are where he once was. He is now helping others discover the very same hope and restoration that changed his life.

As you read this book, I pray you are encouraged, challenged, and reminded that God is still in the business of changing lives. Brent's story is living proof.

—Klayton Kirkwood
Center Director, Teen Challenge of Arizona – Tucson

Chapter One

I never planned to end up in recovery. Nobody does. You don't sit around as a kid and dream of rock bottom. You don't imagine yourself waking up in places you don't remember going to or hurting people you love just to silence the war in your own soul. But that's where I found myself—on the edge of something that looked like the end but would turn out to be the beginning of everything.

When I was a kid, I wanted to be somebody. A firefighter. A soldier. A hero in someone's eyes. I dreamed of saving lives, not trying to salvage the broken pieces of my own. I pictured a house with a porch swing, a dog in the yard, and a family who knew I'd always come home. What I got instead was a front row seat to chaos.

Addiction doesn't show up like a monster. It walks slowly, like a friend offering relief. It doesn't come roaring down your street with a warning—it shows up in whispers, in temptations, in promises of peace that turn into chains. And somewhere between the first high and the thousandth heartbreak, I lost myself. My dreams were replaced by nightmares, my porch swing by a jail cot, and that family I dreamed of? I couldn't even look them in the eye.

I used to say I was in control. But the truth is, control was the first thing I lost. What followed was years of spiraling—moments that blurred together into a mess of regrets and apologies I didn't always mean. I built habits of hiding, routines out of running. You'd be amazed how easy it becomes to lie to yourself when you've lied to everyone else for so long.

And then came the crash. Rock bottom. Or what felt like it. But rock bottom, I've learned, has layers. Every time you think you've reached the bottom, the floor opens beneath you.

I was in a car, pulled over on a Tennessee back road with meth in the glove box and a thousand thoughts racing through my head. Flashing lights. The click of handcuffs. The realization that this might be it. Not just legally— but life-wise. I wasn't scared of jail. I was scared of dying like this—scared that this was how my story would end.

I can still feel the cold steel on my wrists, the way the backseat of that cruiser smelled like stale sweat and cigarettes. I remember staring out the window thinking, is this really all there is for me? My heart pounded, not just from fear, but from the loud echo of shame that finally had no place left to hide.

They say you have to hit bottom before you can look up. I didn't just hit it—I face-planted into it. I remember sitting in a cell, staring at the wall, wondering how the boy who once prayed to be used by God had become a man praying not to wake up. That kind of darkness doesn't lift easily. But in that dark place, God started whispering.

Not in a loud, thunderous voice—but in a quiet, unrelenting one. One that said, "You're not done yet."

And I wasn't.

The day I walked into Teen Challenge, I felt like I was walking into a courtroom, waiting for judgment. My head was down. My spirit was crushed. And everything in me wanted to turn around and run. But something—maybe God, maybe desperation—kept my feet moving.

I was greeted by a staff member who looked me in the eyes like he already knew my story. No words, just a nod. I wanted to scream, "Don't get your hopes up. I'm not staying long." But I didn't. I couldn't. My mouth didn't move, but my soul was groaning.

Everything in the place felt foreign. The songs. The smiles. The prayers. The hope. I didn't trust it. I didn't trust myself. But somewhere deep down, I hoped maybe this would be different.

The first meal I had there, I barely touched. Not because the food was bad—because I felt like I didn't deserve to eat. My hands shook. My stomach twisted. My shame was louder than my hunger.

That night, as I lay in a strange bed with a plastic mattress and a blanket that smelled like bleach, I cried silently. Not out of fear—but exhaustion. It felt like my soul had been carrying a weight for decades and had just put it down for the first time.

And in that silence, I heard something deeper than my fear. I heard hope. Not loud. Just a whisper. But it was enough.

I remember it clearly—day three. A guy shared his story in chapel. He spoke about losing his kids, burying his brother, waking up in an alley covered in blood. And there he was, arms raised, tears streaming, thanking Jesus.

Something cracked in me.

I didn't fall on my knees. I didn't shout Hallelujah. But for the first time in years, I felt something. Empathy. Conviction. Maybe even hope. I realized I wasn't alone in my wreckage. Other men had crawled through their own hell—and found light.

That was the first moment I stopped plotting my escape. I started wondering... what if God could do that for me, too?

Later that night, I asked if I could pray. Just a simple prayer. "God, if You're real, don't let me leave the same." I didn't feel fireworks. But I felt peace. And peace was a miracle to me.

The truth is, I had built my life around numbing the pain, pretending to be okay, and wearing a mask for everyone—including myself. But in this place, with these people, I couldn't hide anymore. And as scary as that was... it was also freeing.

For the first time in years, I could tell the truth. I could say, "I'm not okay," and no one flinched. No one judged me. They nodded like they'd said it themselves, probably just last week. There was something sacred in that shared brokenness.

One night in our dorm room, my bunkmate looked over and said, "You don't have to be strong here. Just be real." That sentence stayed with me. Real beats strong every time.

We'd sit on plastic chairs in a circle, guys with pasts darker than mine, and somehow laughter would break through. Stories that should've ended in tombstones became testimonies. I started to believe in possibility again.

I remember one guy sharing how he had tried to end his life three times. Now he was leading worship. Another had lost his kids but was getting visitation again. We weren't just recovering—we were reclaiming pieces of ourselves we thought were gone for good.

But healing didn't come easy.

There were moments I wanted to quit. Days I sat in chapel with my arms crossed and my heart closed. Nights I laid in bed staring at the ceiling wondering if I'd ever really change. I'd hear worship music and feel nothing. I'd read scripture and feel judged.

I wrestled with shame. With guilt. With the voice in my head that said, "You're too far gone."

But something—or Someone—kept whispering to me, "Keep going. I'm not done with you yet."

God wasn't looking for me to clean myself up before I came to Him. He was ready to meet me in my worst, love me in my lowest, and carry me even when I didn't believe I deserved it. That kind of love? It'll wreck you in the best way.

I started journaling, even when I didn't know what to say. I'd write out prayers that felt more like groans. I'd pace during morning devotions, afraid to sit still with my thoughts. But slowly, something started shifting.

I began to remember who I was before the meth, before the masks, before the mess. Not the addict. Not the convict. But the son. The child of God.
It didn't all change overnight. There were no lightning bolts or fire from the sky. It was slow. Quiet. A smile one day. A prayer the next. A moment of peace where anxiety used to live. One step forward, even when I stumbled the next day.

One morning, I woke up and didn't feel dread. That felt like a miracle.

Another day, I laughed—really laughed—at something one of the guys said. And I realized I hadn't laughed like that in years. Not the fake laugh I used to wear like a costume. A real one. It felt like something sacred broke loose in my chest.

I found myself starting to believe again. Not just in God, but in the idea that I had purpose. That I could still be a father. A friend. A man of God.

I wrote a letter to my son and didn't tear it up this time. I actually mailed it. I asked for forgiveness without making excuses.

I prayed out loud in a group. I raised my hands in worship for the first time. I memorized a scripture that I clung to like a lifeline. I began to look people in the eye again.

Over time, I started to see it—I wasn't just surviving anymore. I was healing.

This was more than recovery.

This was resurrection.

💬 Reflection Prompt:

What masks have you been wearing to hide your pain? What would it look like to let someone see the real you—and to let God begin healing the parts you've been protecting?

Take 5 minutes. Be honest. Be raw. God already knows—He's just waiting for you to invite Him in.

📖 Scripture:Ezekiel 36:26 (KJV)"A new heart also will I give you, and a new spirit will I put within you: and I will take away the stony heart out of your flesh, and I will give you a heart of flesh."

Flashback Chapter

The First Knock

It was February 2020—right before the world shut down.

A time no one will soon forget. But for me, it was unforgettable for reasons far deeper than a virus.

I was sleeping on the floor of a friend's bedroom at her dad's house, strung out and sinking fast.

By day, I was a shift manager at McDonald's.

By night, I was a full-time addict.

I was getting high in the bathroom between cars in the drive-thru. Functioning, barely. Dying, quietly.

Then one day, a friend of mine—who was in prison at the time—invited me to church.

I remember being confused. I was like, "How am I gonna go to church with you when you're locked up?"

He said, "I'll send you a link."

And sure enough, that Sunday morning, he sent me a Facebook Live stream.

I clicked the link… and I don't think I blinked for the entire hour.

I wept through the whole service. I couldn't explain it—but I felt something.

More than that—I felt Someone.

The Spirit of God moved over my body like a wave crashing through years of numbness.

And I couldn't get enough. I watched the next week. Then the next. And the next.

Eventually, my friend told me that the pastor I had been watching was his dad.

I couldn't believe it.

His dad was Pastor Tim—preaching live every week so his son and other men behind bars could still receive the Word of God.

I eventually reached out and messaged him. I just wanted to say thank you. But one message turned into a conversation. And that conversation turned into a relationship. And before long, I found myself pouring out everything—the addiction, the fear, the brokenness.

And Pastor Tim didn't flinch.

He ministered to me like no one ever had. He saw me. And he believed in what could still be.

He told me, "If you're serious about making a change… I know a guy that knows a guy."

That's when I met Timothy.

We talked for a day or two, and he said if I was really ready to change my life, he had a buddy who ran a faith-based rehab near Myrtle Beach. Now, anybody who knows me knows how I feel about the beach—so I paid attention.

Then came Jimbo.

An ex-Hells Angel biker, covered in tattoos, long hair, and a Harley louder than a thunderstorm. I didn't know what to think at first. But I knew this was it.

I had hit the bottom. And I needed out.

Pastor Tim bought me a bus ticket and said, "Just get on that bus, Brent. Just get on."

I was terrified. I had no idea where I was going or who I'd be around.

And Tim later told me he honestly didn't think I'd go through with it.

But that Saturday afternoon—I got on the bus.
And I didn't look back.

Nine hours later, I pulled into the Myrtle Beach station. A drive that should've taken four, but every minute felt like a year. A guy was there to meet me and take me to The Farm.

My head was spinning the whole way. What am I doing? What if this is a mistake?

But when I got there—I was met by something unexpected.

Jimbo.
His loving wife, Mrs. Lynn.
And a group of men who greeted me like I already mattered.

This wasn't a facility. This was a home.

And for the first time in a long time, I didn't feel like a project.
I felt like a person.

Life at the F.R.E.E. Ministry farm on Church Road in Green Sea, South Carolina was nothing like what I was used to.

Every day started at 5 a.m.
Bed made. Dressed. Ready for breakfast.
Then Bible study at 6 a.m.—mandatory.
And not a day passed without reading Proverbs.

After that, it was work on the farm. Real work. Purposeful work.

We tore down old houses and used the materials to build tiny homes for people in need.

We cleaned. We planted. We fixed things that were broken—just like God was doing with us.

Jimbo also pastored a small church just down the road, which used to be a poker house, now turned sanctuary.

We ate together. Worshiped together.

And every Saturday night, we had service—just us and the Spirit.

Then COVID hit.

The world outside shut down—but the Farm kept going.

And I saw it for what it was: a shield.

God had put me in that place for such a time as this.

The brothers I lived with became family.

Jimbo and Mrs. Lynn became like second parents.

Jimbo was rough around the edges, but exactly the kind of leader I needed.

And Mrs. Lynn—she was pure grace.

Soft-spoken. Wise. Faithful. The kind of woman who could make a man believe again.

She taught me 2 Corinthians 10:5—"Take every thought captive…"— and I still carry that to this day.

I started to thrive.

I became the main cook for all the guys. I loved cooking for them—and they loved eating it.

I took over intake duties—processing new arrivals, showing them around.

And I started something I never thought I'd do: college.

I enrolled to begin my Bachelor's in Psychology.
Jimbo believed in me enough to let me start that journey right there on the farm.

F.R.E.E. Ministry had become my home.

But addiction has a voice.
And sometimes, even when you're healing—it still whispers.

I met a guy at the grocery store who I later found out sold crack cocaine.

And that was the beginning of the end.

I started isolating. Using again.
Right there. In the same place God had rescued me.
I felt ashamed. I felt like a fraud.
I didn't know how to face Jimbo or Mrs. Lynn.

So I ran.

Called my friend Summer. She lived in Florida. She didn't ask questions. She just came.

And one day, while everyone was gone, I packed my things and left.
No goodbyes. Just shame.

I made my way to Florida, and Summer—being the loyal friend she is—let me stay.
And I'm forever grateful for her kindness.
We're still close to this day.

But I still carry that year on the farm in my heart.

I still carry them.

Jimbo and Mrs. Lynn didn't just house me.
They loved me.

They believed in me when I didn't believe in myself.
They showed me what it meant to serve, to build, to belong.

Mrs. Lynn and I would sing together on Saturday nights.
We'd garden. Talk. Pray.

She helped me see my purpose.
She helped me remember that God doesn't just rescue—He restores.

I'll never forget her.
And I'll never forget the man God used to get me there.

If you or someone you love is lost—truly lost—please reach out to Jimbo.
F.R.E.E. Ministry will meet you where you are.
Because they met me where I was.

Here's their website:
👉 https://freeministry.net

Jimbo and Mrs. Lynn Boudreau—thank you.
I love you both more than words can say.

God used you to redirect the course of my life forever.
And I will never forget the knock that started it all.

💬 Reflection Prompt:
Have you ever looked back and realized a "failed" season was actually where God started something sacred?
What seeds were planted in your past that are bearing fruit today?

📖 Scripture:
2 Corinthians 10:5 (NIV) – "We demolish arguments and every pretension that sets itself up against the knowledge of God, and we take captive every thought to make it obedient to Christ."

Isaiah 43:19 (ESV) – "Behold, I am doing a new thing… I will make a way in the wilderness and rivers in the desert."

Chapter Two

Before the breakthrough came the breakdown.

There was a time when I could feel everything slipping, but I kept pretending like I had it all under control. I wore confidence like a costume—smiles that didn't reach my eyes, jokes that covered pain, and a hustle mentality that masked how hollow I really felt. But inside? I was unraveling. Quietly. Constantly.

It's a special kind of torment when your insides don't match your outside. I could walk into a room and make people laugh, shake hands, flash a smile. But I'd go home and feel like I was drowning in silence. I could be surrounded by people and still feel utterly alone. I told myself I was managing, that I had a grip on everything. But the truth? Meth had the grip on me.

I didn't want to admit I needed help. That felt weak. That felt like failure. So, I pretended. I worked harder, acted tougher, avoided any moment that would force me to slow down and face the ache inside me. I numbed it with distractions—booze, lies, women, sleep, more meth. It wasn't just a drug anymore. It was a lifestyle. A survival tactic. My escape, my comfort, my god.

I had danced with meth off and on for over 20 years. But I wasn't dancing anymore. I was chained. The high was never high enough. The crash was always deeper. My mind was a maze of paranoia and regret, and my soul was so numb I forgot what it meant to feel.

And when the numbness didn't work anymore, I started looking for ways to make it all stop. Not just the pain. Everything.

There were nights I sat in dark rooms with a loaded gun, hand shaking, heart racing, wondering if anyone would even notice I was gone. I stared at the barrel like it was a doorway to peace. One pull and the noise would end. The shame, the guilt, the torment—gone. I imagined the silence that would follow and thought maybe it would be better than the chaos I was living in.

Other times it wasn't a gun. It was a handful of pills. Or driving faster than I should've around a bend I wasn't sure I'd make it through. Or laying on the floor in the pitch dark, hoping I just wouldn't wake up the next day. Suicidal thoughts weren't visitors—they were roommates. They lived with me. Whispered to me. Made suggestions like old friends.

I wrote notes I never sent. Apologies I never delivered. I stood on the edge more times than I can count—emotionally, mentally, spiritually. And every time, something held me back. A memory of my son's laugh. A song lyric I couldn't shake. A picture on the wall. A whisper in my spirit that said, "Not yet."

There was one night I'll never forget. I was parked at an overlook, way out in the middle of nowhere. The city lights flickered far below, and the meth in my veins made everything buzz except my soul, which felt like a dead battery. I had my hand on the trigger and a tear on my cheek. I whispered, "God, if You're real, this is Your last chance."

And He answered. Not in a voice I could hear, but in the fact that I didn't pull it. I sat there for hours, shaking, crying, breathing. Still alive.

After that, I started seeing death differently. It wasn't just an escape—it was an enemy I had mistakenly believed was my friend. Death didn't want to comfort me. It wanted to erase me. And God wasn't trying to punish me—He was trying to preserve me. I just couldn't see it yet.

The spiral got faster, darker, and heavier. I stopped answering calls. I canceled plans I had no intention of keeping. I avoided eye contact with the people I loved. Not because I didn't love them—but because I was ashamed. I didn't want to be seen like that. I didn't want them to see how far gone I really was.

There's something terrifying about waking up one day and realizing you don't recognize the person in the mirror. You see your face, but not your fire. You speak, but you don't even believe your own words. It's like you're alive but not living—just surviving the fallout of your own choices. I became a ghost with a pulse.

And then came Tennessee.

Just another drive, another day, another weight of meth in the car like it was normal. But it wasn't normal—it was a slow-motion crash I couldn't stop. The blue lights lit up behind me, and I knew in that moment... it was over.

The arrest was humiliating. I can still feel the shame burning on my skin like a rash I couldn't scrub off. I remember the officer's face as he opened the glove box and found what I was hiding. The silence in that moment screamed louder than any siren. There was no excuse. No talking my way out. My lies had expired.

But it was in that cold, lifeless space between the cuffs and the courtroom that God was already preparing the rescue plan I didn't ask for. Because grace doesn't wait for you to ask politely. Grace shows up like a wrecking ball and starts rebuilding what you thought was beyond repair.

But before I go any further, I need to stop and talk about the man who helped make this whole thing happen.

Actually—two men.

Because if it weren't for my attorney, Mr. McCabe, and a man of God named Pastor Russell Coffey, I wouldn't be standing here telling you this story.

Mr. McCabe didn't treat me like a case number. He didn't just argue my charges—he fought for my future.

He saw that prison wasn't going to change me—but maybe redemption could.

At first, he was trying to get me into a rehab there in Tennessee. That alone was more than I expected.

But then—out of nowhere—he said, "You know what? I could make a call to someone I know who helps send people to Teen Challenge. It's in Arizona."

I said, "Hell no."

Across the country?

To a place called Teen Challenge? I was in my 40s. I thought it sounded ridiculous.

But the more he talked… the more I listened.

That's when Pastor Russell Coffey entered the picture.

This man is heaven sent. No doubt about it.

While I sat in that cold, damp jail cell, Pastor Russell and Mr. McCabe were on the outside making moves.

Connecting with my mom. Coordinating the details. Praying over the process.

They handled the logistics and the spiritual warfare.

And somehow—by the grace of God—it all came together.

From a cell with no freedom…

To a seat on a plane headed to Arizona…

To the doors of Teen Challenge…

To a life I never imagined I could have.

I'll never forget what they did for me.

Not just legally—but spiritually.

They didn't just give me a second chance—they gave me a bridge to walk into God's will.

I am eternally grateful for those two men.

Mr. McCabe, for believing in me when most wouldn't.
And Pastor Coffey, for answering the call when God put my name on his heart.

I didn't sign up for Teen Challenge. I was sent. Court-ordered. "Get clean or do time." That was the choice. And to be honest, I was angry. Bitter. I didn't want to be there. I didn't think it would help. I thought it was just another system that wouldn't work. Another box to check. Another letdown waiting to happen.

I showed up mad at the world. Mad at myself. Mad at God. I sat in chapel with arms crossed. I mouthed the prayers. I rolled my eyes at the praise reports. I judged the guys who seemed "too spiritual." I thought, this is fake… this is forced… this is not for me.

But God… oh, man. God had other plans.

He didn't wait for me to get on board. He didn't need me to be "ready" or "willing." He just met me right where I was—ticked off, broken, skeptical, and numb—and He started doing what only He can do.

Little by little, that wall I built up started cracking. Not with explosions. With whispers.

At first, I just went through the motions. Sat through chapel. Showed up to groups. Did what I had to. But somewhere in the middle of that routine, something sacred started to break through.

A moment of peace in the chaos.
A connection with another guy who'd been through it too.
A song in worship that hit too close to home.

A scripture I couldn't shake.

A tear I didn't expect.

A whisper in my spirit: "You belong here. I'm not done with you yet."

I remember one night in particular. I couldn't sleep. The room was quiet except for the sound of someone else snoring across the dorm. I sat up, put my feet on the cold tile floor, and just whispered, "God… what now?"

And I felt it. Not lightning. Not thunder. Just presence. Peace. A warmth I hadn't felt in years. The kind that says, "I see you. I haven't forgotten you."

That night, I cried. Not out of frustration. But because something in me cracked open. And for once, I didn't try to patch it up. I let it break. And in that breaking, God started building.

The next morning, I actually listened during devotion. I picked up a Bible and read a full chapter for the first time in years. The words didn't just sit on the page—they stirred something in me. I wasn't healed yet, but the healing had begun.

What started as a sentence became a sanctuary. I didn't just need to be here—I wanted to be here. And not just to get sober. I wanted to be healed. To be whole. To be new.

It still wasn't easy. There were days I wanted to run. Days I questioned everything. Days I doubted whether I was really changing or just pretending again. But deep inside, I started to believe that maybe—just maybe—God could still use me. That I wasn't too far gone. That grace really does reach into the darkest corners and says, "Let there be light."

And that light? It was flickering now. Not a flame yet, but it was there.

And for the first time in a long time, I had hope.

💬 Reflection Prompt:

What's the moment in your life where things felt like they were truly falling apart? Can you see how, even in that mess, God was already making a way for healing?

Write about a time you thought was the end—but it turned out to be a beginning.

📖 Scripture:

Psalm 40:2 (KJV)"He brought me up also out of a horrible pit, out of the miry clay, and set my feet upon a rock, and established my goings."

Chapter Three

There's something strange that happens when you stop running.

It doesn't happen all at once. It's not like you suddenly throw up your hands and say, "Okay, God, I'm ready," and everything just clicks into place. No, it's slower than that. Clumsier. Messier. But somewhere in the routine, in the structure, in the stillness, you realize... you're changing.

That's what Teen Challenge became for me. A forge. A furnace. A place where everything that had been twisted, scarred, and shattered in my life started to get reshaped—not by force, but by faith.

...

I used to look at other men and think, "I'll never be like that." Not because I didn't want to be good, but because I genuinely believed I didn't have it in me. I thought I was born broken. Destined to fall short. But somewhere between the Bible studies and the early morning chores, God began to whisper something new: You're not too far gone.

There was a morning where I felt it the strongest. I was assigned to sweep the sidewalks, and it had just rained. The air was cool and heavy, and I could see my breath. I paused, leaned on my broom, and for a moment, I was overwhelmed by peace. Real peace. Not chemically-induced. Not forced. Just... stillness.

In that stillness, I looked up and saw the sky breaking open with the rising sun. The clouds glowed orange and pink, and something in me softened. For so many years, I had cursed the mornings. I hated waking up. But now, for the first time in decades, I looked forward to it. I didn't know what the day would bring, but I was no longer dreading it. I was meeting it. With open hands.

That, to me, was proof of a miracle.

My mornings turned into sacred time. I'd sneak out with my Bible and journal while the rest of the dorm still slept. The silence wasn't empty anymore—it was holy. God started speaking in the simplest ways. A verse that felt like it was written just for me. A bird landing on the bench next to me. A memory I hadn't visited in years that suddenly held new meaning.

One morning I read Psalm 34:18: "The Lord is close to the brokenhearted and saves those who are crushed in spirit." I stopped. I read it again. And again. Tears welled up. I knew He was close. I could feel Him.

And here's the thing—I didn't get some supernatural vision or audible voice. I got something better: presence. A tangible awareness that I wasn't alone. That I was finally home, not just in a building, but in my soul.

My conversations with God stopped sounding like formal prayers and started sounding like the realest parts of me. I talked to Him like a Father. A Friend. Sometimes I just sat and cried. Sometimes I laughed and told Him what I was grateful for. Sometimes I confessed the dark stuff I was too afraid to tell anyone else. And every time, He met me there.

I found healing in service too. One night, a new guy came in strung out, eyes full of fear and anger. I sat with him for two hours. Didn't say much—just listened. When he finally opened up, he said, "You don't judge me. Why?" And I said, "Because I am you."

That's when I knew God wasn't just healing me for me. He was healing me so I could help heal others.

I started leading short devotions. I was nervous at first—hands sweating, voice cracking. But the more I spoke, the more I realized something: my story had power. Not because I had it all figured out, but because I didn't. Because I was honest about the pain and bold about the redemption. Because I didn't sugarcoat the struggle.

One of my favorite devotion moments was when I shared about the prodigal son. I said, "Some of us think we have to clean ourselves up before we come back to the Father. But the son was still dirty, still smelling like pigs, and the Father ran to him anyway."

You could feel the atmosphere shift. Some guys wept. Others stared blankly, like they'd never heard the gospel that way. That was the day I realized: I'm not just being restored. I'm becoming a restorer.

Another defining moment came during our 24-hour prayer event. Each guy signed up for an hour of prayer. Mine was at 3 a.m. I was groggy, but I showed up. The room was dim. Worship music played low. I sat on the floor and whispered, "Lord, I don't even know what to say right now."

What followed was an hour of deep, gut-level connection. I prayed for my family. I prayed for the people I hurt. I prayed for the young version of me who got so lost. I prayed for the future me—whoever he'd become.

And then I just sat in silence. Not awkward silence. Sacred silence. I felt God's love like a blanket wrapped around my soul. Gentle. Heavy. Secure.

That hour changed everything.

By the time my prayer shift ended, I didn't want to leave. I stayed another hour just worshiping. That night, I felt like I saw a glimpse of who I was always meant to be—a worshiper. A warrior. A witness.

I was starting to dream again.

I used to avoid dreams because they reminded me of what I thought I could never have. But now, I was dreaming with God. About being a father who shows up. A leader who lifts others. A man who walks in light, not shame.

And for the first time in my life, I believed those dreams weren't just fantasies. They were promises.

So yes—transformation came in layers. In chapel. In journaling. In serving. In grief. In grace. In forgiveness. In silence. In sweat. In tears. In sunrise. In scripture. In surrender.

And that's when I truly understood what it meant to be made new— not just improved. New.

💬 Reflection Prompt:
What's something broken in your past that God is beginning to restore? Where in your life are you no longer just surviving—but beginning to become who you were created to be?
Take a moment. Let God speak into that space.

▢ Scripture:
2 Corinthians 5:17 (KJV)"Therefore if any man be in Christ, he is a new creature: old things are passed away; behold, all things are become new."

Chapter Four

Before the meth.
Before the handcuffs.
Before the courtroom, the recovery, the resurrection...
There was a boy.

A boy who learned early that love could vanish without warning.
That safety wasn't promised.
That the people who were supposed to protect you sometimes just... didn't.
That boy was me.

It started with something as simple as a summer visit.
My mom sent me and my sister to spend a few months with our dad. Maybe she needed a break. Maybe she believed he'd step up. But he didn't.
He left us.
Just took off to the races—gone.
No food. No goodbye. Just two little kids sitting in a house with empty cupboards and empty stomachs, waiting for someone who wasn't coming back.

I remember wandering the neighborhood—barefoot, hungry, and desperate—knocking on doors, begging strangers for food. Not snacks. Not candy. Just something—anything—to survive.
Eventually, the system stepped in.
And just like that, we were sent to the children's home.
But it wasn't a home.
Not for us.

It was a prison with metal bedframes.

Too many kids. Too little love. Too many rules. Too few arms to hold the hurting.

And at night, the real terror would come.

I'd lie there in bed—tiny, fragile, pretending to be asleep—while the walls betrayed their secrets. From the next room, I'd hear it.

Cries. Pleading. Whispers turning into screams.

"Please stop." "No." "Don't."

The sound of innocence being ripped from another child—and I'd freeze, tears streaming down my face, heart pounding in my chest.

Because I knew my turn was coming.

The fear wasn't in what was happening—it was in the waiting.

The knowing.

The helplessness of hearing it happen to someone else, unable to stop it… and the soul-crushing knowledge that the same pain was walking straight toward my door.

No child should ever feel that.

No child should ever have to prepare for trauma like it's part of their bedtime routine.

But I did.

And the worst part?

I thought it was my fault.

That's the twisted lie abuse tells you. That if your dad had stayed, or if you'd been stronger, or if you hadn't asked for food, none of this would've happened.

That lie settled in my bones.

And I carried it for decades.

So, I stopped trusting.

Stopped hoping.

Stopped needing.

And when I found meth?

It didn't judge me.

Didn't ask questions.

Didn't care where I came from or what I was running from.

It just offered silence.

And for a long time, that's all I wanted—to not hear the cries anymore. Not in the room next door. Not in my head. Not in my heart.

But there's more I need you to understand.

Because the impact of that trauma didn't just shape who I became—it shaped who I couldn't become. It robbed me of childhood joys, the ability to laugh freely, to trust without reservation, to believe that the world could be safe. I would see other kids riding bikes, playing tag, wrapped in the arms of parents who seemed to actually care. And I'd think, "Why not me?"

I learned early how to wear a mask. To be charming when necessary. To act like I was fine. But inside? I was a storm. Unseen. Unheard. Unwanted. And that kind of storm doesn't just pass—it brews. It builds. Until one day, it explodes.

And mine did. In the form of addiction. Anger. Violence. Self-hate. Every choice I made in rebellion was a desperate scream that said, "Don't forget me. Don't ignore me. I'm still here!"

But people didn't hear the scream. They only saw the mess.

And it made sense to them. The arrests. The relapses. The pain I caused. They thought it was all my doing.

But if they could have seen the little boy still trapped inside me, begging for someone to just care enough to ask why—I wonder if they'd have responded differently.

I'm not blaming everything I did on my past. I made choices. I hurt people. I own that.

But I also know that much of my chaos came from untreated trauma, from wounds so deep they bled into every corner of my life.

There's a detail I've never shared until now. One night, after it had happened again, I snuck into the bathroom, locked the door, and stared at myself in the mirror. I didn't cry. I didn't scream. I just stared. Because even as a child, I knew something inside me had died. And I was mourning it without even knowing how.

I remember pressing my hands into my face, trying to push the pain back inside.
Trying to be brave.
Trying to pretend I hadn't just been broken again.

It's moments like that—quiet, invisible, devastating—that never leave you.
They become part of your wiring.
They shape your instincts.
They become the reasons you build walls so high no one can climb them.

I share this now not for pity, but for purpose.
Because I know there are others like me.
Men and women carrying stories too heavy to speak out loud.
Wounds they're still bleeding from decades later.
People who still wait at night, afraid of footsteps they haven't heard in years, but that echo through their memories.

To you, I say: you are not alone.
You are not crazy.
And your healing is not impossible.

I remember the day I finally told my mom what had happened.
It took everything in me.
I was a grown man, but I felt like that little boy again.
Ashamed. Scared. Unsure if I'd be believed.
But I couldn't carry it alone anymore.

And when I finally spoke it out loud, something shifted.
Not everything was fixed. Not all the pain vanished.
But the silence was shattered.
And that's where healing begins.

Every time I share my story now, I feel that same fear rise up. But I do it anyway.

Because someone has to.

Because too many boys become broken men who never learn how to mend.

Because too many girls grow into women who still flinch at love because of what was done to them in the dark.

But Jesus.

He steps into that dark.

He walks into those locked rooms.

He sits with the child we used to be and says, "I saw it. I was there. And I'm still here."

So if you're reading this and your heart is racing because you know this pain—I speak this over you now:

Your voice matters.

Your story matters.

And your healing is possible.

I am not who I am today because the pain disappeared.

I am who I am today because I let God step into it.

I let Him sit with me in the mess.

And slowly—so slowly—it became something sacred.

Not because it was good.

But because He is.

That's the miracle.

Not that we forget what happened.

But that we can live fully anyway.

That we can tell the truth and not be swallowed by it.

That we can walk into rooms with our heads high, carrying stories once too heavy to speak.

So here I am.

Not a victim.

Not just a survivor.
But a voice.
A warrior.
A man with scars that scream, "God is real. God is good. And God redeems."

Because the waiting is over.
And I'm not afraid of the night anymore.

And maybe most importantly—I'm not hiding anymore. Not from the truth. Not from my past. Not from the pain. I've found the strength to stand in the light, even when my voice shakes. I've found the courage to speak for that little boy who didn't have a voice back then. I speak for him now. I fight for him now. I live for him now.

So if you're out there—still scared, still quiet, still waiting—know this: your story matters. Your truth matters. And God is big enough to carry it all. The wounds. The silence. The rage. The questions. Bring it all to Him. He's not afraid of your broken pieces. He builds beauty with them.

◯ Reflection Prompt:
What pain have you been carrying that wasn't your fault—but still shaped your life?
What would it look like to give God access to that room—the one you've kept locked all these years?
Be honest. Be brave. The healing starts where the hiding ends.

▢ Scripture:
Romans 8:18 (KJV)
"For I reckon that the sufferings of this present time are not worthy to be compared with the glory which shall be revealed in us."

Chapter Five

They say healing isn't linear, and that's the truth.

I wish I could say that after my walls broke and my past spilled out, everything got easier. But that's not how it works. The light doesn't come in without first burning through the dark.

After all the trauma I carried, after the years of meth and madness, after surviving what should've destroyed me—I stood in a place built for transformation, and I had a choice:

Let God rebuild me… or keep pretending I was fine.

And brother, I was tired of pretending.

At this point in Teen Challenge, I wasn't new anymore. I wasn't the guy staring at the floor in the back row or sneaking out mentally during chapel. I had started showing up—really showing up.

And the crazy thing?

God met me in the showing up.

Not just in the worship or the Bible studies. But in the mundane, the daily rhythms—the early morning chores, the meals we served, the guys I talked with after lights-out when the walls came down and the real stuff came out.

That's where I began to understand:

Healing isn't always a miracle moment. Sometimes it's a slow becoming.

I remember one night; I was wiping down tables in the cafeteria after dinner. Just a normal night. But something hit me—I was at peace.

No high. No escape. No false comfort.

Just… peace.

That moment stopped me. Because for so long, I thought peace came from silence, from checking out, from numbing. But this was different.

This was presence.

God was with me, right there between the rag and the leftover crumbs.

And He whispered in my heart:
"See? You don't need the drugs. You just need Me."
That broke me again.
But this time, it was a beautiful breaking. A surrender.

The leadership started noticing.
I started leading morning devos. Helping the new guys. Sharing my story little by little. Not the polished version—but the real, raw, God's-still-working-on-me version.

And for the first time in a long time, I didn't feel like a fraud.
I felt like a man becoming who he was always meant to be.

But let me be real—it wasn't all peace and praise.
There were still days the enemy whispered:
"You'll never be free."
"You're faking it."
"Your past is too big."
Some days, I believed it.
Some days, I almost gave up.

There were mornings I'd wake up with a heaviness I couldn't explain. The kind of weight that made getting out of bed feel like a battle. I'd question everything—why God had chosen me, why I was still struggling, whether any of this was real. And in those moments, I had to learn how to fight differently.

Not with my fists. Not with hiding. But with faith.

Some mornings, my prayers were nothing more than groans. Just a whispered, "Help me, God." And somehow, that was enough. Somehow, grace met me even in my weakest confession.

It was in those moments—those unspoken, unseen battles—that I was being shaped. Not in the spotlight, but in the shadows. Not in the victories, but in the valleys.

Community became my mirror. The brothers around me reflected truth I couldn't yet see in myself. They challenged me, checked me, encouraged me, prayed over me, called me out, lifted me up. We weren't just roommates—we were warriors in recovery, linked arm in arm.

We'd sit on the porch late at night and talk about our regrets, our hopes, our fears. We'd laugh at stupid jokes, cry over hard memories, and pray like our lives depended on it—because they did. Those porch conversations? They were holy ground.

Sometimes healing looked like doing someone else's dishes without being asked. Sometimes it looked like holding back harsh words and choosing kindness. Sometimes it looked like just staying put when every bone in your body wanted to run.

I started journaling like my life depended on it. I filled notebooks with prayers, thoughts, letters to the old me, letters to my son, letters to God. Some of those entries were angry. Some were confused. But all of them were honest. And honesty, I learned, is the birthplace of transformation.

I remember one entry clearly. It simply read:
"Lord, I don't know how to do this. But I trust You. Teach me how to be new."

And day by day, He did.

I saw it in the way I started to speak differently.
I saw it in how I looked people in the eyes instead of looking down.
I saw it in the way I began to forgive—not just others, but myself.

Forgiveness was hard.
Forgiving myself was brutal.

I had to face the father I wasn't. The promises I broke. The lies I told. The people I hurt. And instead of drowning in shame, I had to hand those memories over to the One who already carried the weight of them.

And God? He didn't reject me. He received me.
Every scar.
Every failure.
Every relapse.
Every wound.

He met me in the mess.
And He started making something beautiful.

I didn't see it all at once. It was more like noticing the sun slowly rising after a long night. First, a little light. Then more. Then warmth. Then vision.

One day, I looked in the mirror, and for the first time, I didn't see a criminal, or a drug addict, or a broken man.
I saw evidence.

Evidence that God takes what's shattered and rebuilds it better than new.
Evidence that mercy still has power.
Evidence that healing is real—even for people like me.

So if you're in the middle of your "becoming," let me say this to you:
Don't give up.
It's not supposed to be easy.
It's supposed to be holy.

You're not behind.
You're becoming.

Every day you show up, even when it's hard.
Every time you choose honesty over hiding.
Every time you ask for help.
Every time you pray one more time.
Every moment you surrender your story to God—He's building something eternal.

He's not rushing you.
He's forming you.

And the world may not see it yet.
But heaven does.
And one day, the evidence will speak for itself.

💬 Reflection Prompt:
Where in your life are you seeing God's presence in the small moments?
What new identity is He revealing to you—not based on your past, but on His promises?

Pause and write it out. You're becoming. Don't rush it.

📖 Scripture:
Philippians 1:6 (KJV)
"Being confident of this very thing, that he which hath begun a good work in you will perform it until the day of Jesus Christ."

Chapter Six

At some point in recovery, things shift.

Not everything's fixed. Not all the scars are healed. But you realize you've been sitting at the feet of grace long enough to start standing. And not just for yourself—for others.

That's what happened to me.
One day I woke up and it hit me:
I wasn't just staying sober anymore… I was walking in freedom.
And freedom always demands that we help somebody else get free too.

I didn't feel ready. I didn't feel qualified. Honestly, I still felt like the same old me on most days. But God started opening doors—little ones at first.

"Hey, can you pray over the guys tonight?"
"Would you be willing to share your story with the new intakes?"
"Can you help with devotions tomorrow morning?"

Every part of me wanted to say, "Who, me?"
But my spirit said, "Yes, Lord."

Because deep down, I knew what it felt like to be the guy walking through those doors for the first time. Lost. Ashamed. Hardened. Skeptical. Starving for hope and too scared to ask for it.

So, I started pouring out what little I had.
And you know what happened?
God multiplied it.

I wasn't preaching sermons—I was just being real.

Telling guys the truth:
That I was court-ordered to be there.
That I came in high, angry, and full of doubt.
That I'd spent years running from everything and everyone—including God.
That I'd heard the screams from the next room as a child and thought I'd never recover.

That meth had its claws in me for over twenty years, and yet here I stood—not perfect, but free.

And when I spoke… I saw something in their eyes.
Hope.

Not the loud kind. Not jumping-out-of-your-seat kind. But the slow-burn kind. The "maybe I'm not too far gone" kind. The "if he can come back from that, maybe I can too" kind.

That's when I realized something big:
My pain had become my platform.
Not because I deserved it. Not because I earned it.
But because God doesn't waste anything.

Every sleepless night.
Every broken bone in my spirit.
Every lie I believed.
Every needle, every high, every desperate prayer I thought He never heard…
He was using all of it.
To reach the broken.
To touch the addicted.
To remind the forgotten that they are still chosen.

I started helping around the center more—taking ownership of responsibilities, serving with joy, showing up early and staying late. Not because I had to… but because I wanted to.

Serving became my healing.

And the wildest part?
The more I gave, the more I got.
The more I poured out; the more God filled me up.
It wasn't just recovery anymore.
It was calling.

But there's more. More to say. More to feel. More to give.

Because I began to realize that healing doesn't just change what you
do—it changes who you are. I didn't even notice it at first. The way I
carried myself was different. My eyes weren't darting around in paranoia.
My shoulders weren't hunched with the shame of my past. My smile—
real, not forced—started showing up more often. It wasn't about
pretending I was fixed. It was about trusting I was being made whole.

One night, I was sitting outside under the stars, just me and God. I
remember whispering, "Lord, I feel different. Am I really changing?" And
I felt His reply—not in thunder, but in a still, undeniable presence:

"Yes, son. You're becoming who I always knew you were."

I wept.

Not from sadness, but from the joy of being seen—finally seen. Not
for my record, not for my failures, but for my identity in Christ. The
addict was dying. The old man was fading. And in his place, a new
creation was rising up.

And that's what drives me now. Not proving people wrong. Not
climbing out of some pit of regret to make a name for myself. But to pour
everything I've received back into those who haven't felt it yet.

You don't have to have it all together to serve.
You just have to be willing to stay.
To show up.

To carry the corner of someone else's mat when they can't walk on their own.

I started leading a small Bible group for new guys. Some of them barely knew scripture. Some didn't want to be there. But I kept showing up, week after week. And little by little, walls came down. Questions were asked. Tears were shed. Faith sparked.

And all the while, I was being ministered to, too. Because when you pour out, you make space to be poured into. That's kingdom math.

I began writing letters—long letters—to men I used to run with. Some locked up. Some lost in the same pit I was delivered from. I didn't preach. I just told them the truth:

"Brother, if you're still breathing, God's not done with you."

Some wrote back.
Some didn't.
But I kept writing.
Because someone once wrote to me.

That's what this is about.
Leaving a trail.
A breadcrumb path of grace for the ones who don't know how to find their way back.

You never know what your yes will unlock for someone else.

Maybe your yes becomes the doorway to their deliverance.
Maybe your obedience is the answer to their prayer.
Maybe your story is the permission they need to start telling their own.

So I keep saying yes.
Yes to the early mornings.
Yes to the hard conversations.
Yes to staying when it would be easier to leave.

Yes to mentoring men who remind me of my darkest days.

Because Jesus didn't save me to sit on the sidelines.
He saved me so I could stand in the trenches with someone else and say, "You don't have to die here."

And when I get tired—and I do—I remember the face of my son.
I remember the men who reached back when I didn't know which way was forward.

I remember that night under the stars.
And I remember the voice that said, "You are mine."

I live for that voice now.

Because when He speaks, everything else goes quiet.

And I will spend the rest of my life making sure the men who walk through these doors never forget they're loved.

Even when they relapse.
Even when they fall.
Even when they feel like all hope is gone.

There's purpose waiting on the other side of that pain.
There's grace big enough for that guilt.
There's a Savior who still says, "Follow Me."

And when they can't walk yet?
I'll carry them.
Until they can.

Because that's what somebody did for me.

And I'll never stop saying thank You... by saying yes.

And maybe, just maybe, one of those men I'm walking beside today will turn around one day and say, "I remember him. He didn't give up on me."

And that—
That will make every step worth it.

And if one day I stand in front of a crowd—or just one man—who says, "Because of you, I didn't give up," I'll know it wasn't because I had the answers, or the strength, or even the perfect recovery story. It'll be because I kept showing up. Because I kept choosing surrender over silence. Because I kept letting my scars speak louder than my shame.

Every cup of coffee shared, every moment I chose to listen instead of fix, every late-night prayer whispered for someone who didn't even know I was praying—that's legacy. That's what matters.

And when I take my last breath on this earth, I won't be holding onto medals or achievements. I'll be holding onto moments. Moments where heaven touched earth because one broken man chose to believe that grace really was enough.

So yes, I'll keep saying yes.
Yes to God.
Yes to grace.
Yes to the next man walking through the fire.
Because that's who I am now.

And I wouldn't trade it for anything.

Because the truth is, I've found more purpose in a mop bucket and a prayer circle than I ever did in chasing money, women, or street respect. I've discovered that healing isn't loud—it's faithful. It's in waking up early to intercede for someone you used to despise. It's in giving up your seat so a broken man can sit in your place, just to feel seen. It's in being the kind of man who shows up when it's inconvenient, when it's messy, when it's thankless.

And I think that's the kind of legacy Jesus left us. Not one of comfort, but of calling. Not one of applause, but of obedience. If I can spend the rest of my days being a bridge for others to walk across—from pain into peace, from addiction into freedom, from shame into identity—then that's enough. That's more than enough.

Because grace didn't just save me. It assigned me. And now every step I take is a step someone else might need to see.

So I'll keep walking.
Even when it's hard.
Even when I'm tired.
Even when the old lies try to creep back in.

Because someone, somewhere, is watching—and wondering if freedom is really possible.

And I want my life to say, without hesitation:
Yes. It is.

💬 Reflection Prompt:
Has God ever used your pain to help someone else?
What's one area of your life you never thought would have purpose—where He might be calling you to serve now?
Think about it. Write it down. Pray on it. There's power in your story.

📖 Scripture:
Genesis 50:20 (KJV)
"But as for you, ye thought evil against me; but God meant it unto good,
to bring to pass, as it is this day, to save many people alive."

The Interlude

I've knocked on more doors than I could ever count.

In the rain, in the heat, with sweat dripping down my back and hope dripping out my spirit. I knocked with shoes worn thin and a pitch worn smoother than my own sense of identity. Neighborhood after neighborhood. Smile after fake smile. Rejection after rejection.

Sometimes I didn't even want the "yes" for the commission. I wanted it for the confirmation—that I was still somebody. That I still existed. That I hadn't completely disappeared into the addiction swallowing me from the inside out.

But you can only be told "no" so many times before it seeps into your bones.

Before the word "no" doesn't just mean no, I don't want what you're selling…
It starts to sound like:
No, you're not worth my time.
No, I don't trust you.
No, I don't believe in you.
No, you're not welcome.

That'll mess with your mind.

You start to see yourself as a nuisance.
An interruption.
A walking inconvenience.

And eventually, you stop knocking just on doors…

You start knocking on your own confidence, hoping something will answer.

I remember entire days where every single door was a no. Not just polite rejections, either.

Doors slammed in my face.
People yelling at me.
Telling me to get a real job.
Telling me to leave their property.
Looking at me like I was dirt.

They didn't know I was already dying inside.
They didn't know I had taken a hit that morning just to stop the shaking.
They didn't know I had a son I wasn't raising and a soul I wasn't facing.

But those rejections didn't care.

Each one chipped away at the fragile scaffolding of my worth.
And over time, the wear and tear on the outside mirrored what was breaking on the inside.

See, rejection doesn't just sting. It echoes.
It builds a voice in your head that starts to sound like your own, whispering lies like:

You'll never be enough.
Nobody wants what you have.
You're not lovable.
You're not seen.

Every no becomes a notch in the belt of shame you wear tighter every day.
Every slammed door becomes another silent sermon preached over your spirit:
"You don't belong."

And yet—I kept knocking.

Not just because I needed the paycheck.
But because something in me refused to fully die.
Some ember still believed there had to be more.

But that belief got buried.

Because addiction + rejection = spiritual starvation.

You're constantly performing.
Constantly proving.
Constantly begging for somebody to validate you.

You're on your feet all day—working, walking, selling—
But your soul is on its knees, begging someone to just say,
"Yes—you matter."

And when you finally do get a sale, that fleeting moment of validation fades fast.

You're back at it again tomorrow. More doors. More no's. More pretending.
And inside, you're slowly forgetting who you even are without the hustle.

I used to believe I was just working hard.
But the truth?
I was auditioning for acceptance.
Every day.

And what I didn't realize is that I wasn't just selling a product—I was selling pieces of myself.

Until one day, there was almost nothing left to sell.

Then came the porch.

That woman. That moment. That sentence.

"You look tired. Like… soul tired."

And it wasn't just what she said—it was how she said it.
Like she saw me—not the salesman, not the addict, not the act—but the broken man underneath it all.

And I couldn't fake it anymore. I couldn't pitch my way out of it.

I turned around and walked away, because for the first time, I felt exposed.
I felt human.
I felt like God had just tapped me on the shoulder and said,
"That's enough. Come home."

But I didn't know how.
Because I'd been gone so long, I forgot what home even felt like.

That's what addiction does.
It doesn't just kill you.
It replaces you.

It turns your dreams into obligations.
Your purpose into a paycheck.
Your story into a script you recite just to survive the day.

And the longer you stay in it, the harder it is to believe that anything different could ever be real.

But here's where grace flipped the script.

God didn't wait for me at a church altar.
He came to the streets.
To the porches.
To the busted cars where I wept.

To the moments I screamed into the silence, begging for a reason not to end it all.

He met me in the knock.

Not when I was ready—but when I was ruined.

And even then—He didn't reject me.
He didn't say, "No thanks."
He didn't shut the door.

He opened it. Wide. With arms. With love. With mercy that makes no sense.

And I finally saw—He'd been on the other side the whole time.

Waiting.

Not with conditions.
Not with judgment.
But with a meal already prepared and a robe already picked out.

Like the prodigal father in the Bible—He wasn't just opening the door.
He was running down the driveway to meet me.

Here's what I've learned:

The world will say no a thousand times before it ever says yes.
And if you base your worth on the world's approval—you'll go mad.

You'll stay in cycles that drain your spirit and destroy your soul.

But when you finally let Jesus open the door of your heart…
You stop knocking for love.
You stop begging for belonging.
You realize—you are the beloved.
You are already home.

But even now, years removed from that hustle, I still think about the people.

Not the customers. Not the ones who bought the product.

I think about the ones I lied to.
The ones I manipulated.
The ones who trusted the man at their doorstep—and got a mask instead.

I wasn't just selling vacuums or deregulated energy. I was selling illusions.
I told half-truths wrapped in charm because I needed that "yes" more than I needed integrity.

And even though I've been forgiven, even though the blood of Jesus has cleansed me—
I still remember their faces.

I'm haunted by the kindness I betrayed.
By the elderly woman who invited me in and gave me water, and I still pushed the pitch.
By the single mom who said she couldn't afford it, and I leaned harder anyway.
By the tired man who just got off work and didn't need a sales pitch—but I gave him one anyway, because I needed that hit.

Those moments revisit me sometimes.

In the quiet.
In my prayers.
In the mirror.

But here's what I've learned:

God doesn't erase our memories—He redeems them.
He lets us remember, not to shame us—but to shape us.

To keep us soft.
To keep us honest.
To keep us humble.

Because I'm not proud of who I was—but I praise the God who met me there.

And I pray that every seed I sow now—through testimony, through truth, through love—is a small act of repair for the damage I once did.

That maybe, somehow, the man who once knocked for profit can now knock on hearts for purpose.

So if you're out there right now...

Still knocking.
Still pretending.
Still hoping that maybe just one more sale, one more fix, one more day will make it better—

Stop.
Take your hand off the next door.

And turn around.

Because He's been knocking on your door the whole time.

And He doesn't want your pitch.
He wants your pain.
He doesn't need your presentation—He wants your presence.

Let Him in.

Not the fake version. Not the polished pitchman.
The real you.

That's the door that changes everything.
That's the door that doesn't just open—it saves.

💬 Final Reflection Prompt:

How has rejection shaped the way you see yourself?

What would change if you let God's yes be louder than the world's no?

📖 Scripture:

Isaiah 41:9-10 (NLT) –

"I have called you back from the ends of the earth, saying, 'You are my servant.' For I have chosen you and will not throw you away. Don't be afraid, for I am with you. Don't be discouraged, for I am your God."

Revelation 3:20 (KJV) –

"Behold, I stand at the door, and knock: if any man hear my voice, and open the door, I will come in to him, and will sup with him, and he with me."

Chapter Seven

But part of that shame I carried wasn't just about my failures as a father—it was also rooted in the ghosts of my past, the people I once ran with, and the place I tried so hard to leave behind: Key Pines.

I grew up in that neighborhood. Played football in the street with boys who would later become addicts, felons, and in some cases... corpses. We were just kids back then. Running barefoot through the summer heat, riding bikes until the streetlights came on, talking about what we'd be when we grew up—none of us realizing that addiction, poverty, and broken homes were already shaping our destinies more than we knew.

I still remember Darnell. Man, that kid could make anybody laugh. He had this way of cracking a joke at the worst time and somehow making it the best time. We used to sneak cigarettes behind the laundromat and talk about what it would be like to get out of Key Pines, to have money, cars, real futures. Last I heard, he OD'd behind a gas station just outside of town. He never made it out.

Then there was Manny. Quiet. Solid. Always watching. He saw things nobody else did. He saw through me before I could even figure myself out. I still hear his voice sometimes when I'm in a rough spot, reminding me who I said I wanted to be. Manny got locked up at 19. Caught a charge he didn't deserve, and the streets never gave him a second chance.

And Marcus... Marcus was like a brother. We did everything together—first time getting high, first time skipping school, first time stealing to get a fix. We laughed, we fought, we cried. He got clean once. Even got a job and started writing music. But the demons came back hard, and one night he just disappeared. They found him two weeks later in an abandoned house, needle still in his arm.

I carry their stories with me. Not as shame anymore—but as reminders. Markers of mercy. Proof that I'm still here, not because I'm better, but because grace intervened. Because where they died, I was delivered. And I refuse to waste that.

I wonder sometimes what they'd think if they could see me now. If they'd believe that Brent—the same one who used to run from everything good—now runs toward God. That I'm not just surviving anymore—I'm speaking life. I'm walking free. I'm breaking chains they never had the chance to.

Key Pines is still with me. It lives in my memory, in my rhythm, in the way I talk to other guys who come from the same streets. I know their language. I know their pain. I know what it's like to grow up thinking you're already doomed. And that makes the message I carry that much louder:

You are not your zip code.
You are not your father's failures.
You are not your past.

You are chosen. You are called. You are still breathing because God is not finished.

And for every kid still growing up in a neighborhood like Key Pines, I want to be a voice that says, "You can rise. You can rebuild. You can be more."

Because by the grace of God… I did.

And then there's Cayce. One of the real ones who stuck by me through it all. She wasn't just a friend—she was a light in a season when I didn't see much worth saving. I've watched her raise her kids with grit and grace, and now I see her pouring into her grandkids with the same fierce love. Through all my darkest chapters, she never turned her back on me. She reminded me of who I was when I couldn't see it for myself. Her friendship has been a constant thread—steady, true, and rooted in love. I thank God for people like her, who reflect His kind of loyalty: unconditional, unwavering, and full of grace.

And then there's Michelle. Her presence in my life has been more than friendship—it's been an anchor. She's seen parts of me most people would run from, but she never flinched. She's been there in my silence, in my chaos, in my fight to rise. Her heart is pure gold—gentle, fierce, and full of the kind of wisdom you don't learn in books. She reminds me that love doesn't always have to be loud to be powerful. Her words have lifted me, her prayers have covered me, and her loyalty has never wavered. She means more to me than words could ever fully say.

And then there's Jaime. Her friendship goes all the way back to when I was just a boy, and I'll never forget what her family did for me. Her mom and dad used to take me to church, back when I didn't even know how badly I needed it. They welcomed me like I was one of their own, and for a kid like me—craving love, craving stability—that meant everything. Jaime and her family became a second home, a safe place in a world that felt anything but safe. She's still in my life to this day, and I count that as one of my biggest blessings. There's a kind of gratitude that never fades, and that's what I carry for her.

And then there's Carrie. She's been a huge part of my life—a steady, compassionate presence through the years. I've watched her raise six amazing kids with fierce love and strength, and I've walked beside her through moments that would break most people. I was there when she lost one of her twin boys in a horrific car accident, and I saw a mother grieve with unimaginable pain—but also with unshakable grace. Carrie's love, her resilience, and her faith in the face of tragedy have inspired me more than words could ever express. I love her deeply. She's family to me, and her strength is a light I always carry with me.

And then there's Ana. She's been in my life since we were young, and her friendship is one of those rare gifts that time can't tarnish. Through every chapter—good, bad, and downright messy—Ana has stayed in my corner. We've laughed until we cried, and cried until we laughed again. She knows where I come from, what I've been through, and somehow never let any of that change the way she's loved me. I've been lucky to have friends I can count on both hands who've walked this life with me—and Ana is one of those lifelong blessings I'll never take for granted.

And then there's Nicole. Watching her rise from addiction to walk in sobriety alongside me has been one of the greatest joys of my journey. She's more than a friend—she's a sister in every way that matters. I love her, her kids, and her mother as if they were my own blood. We've walked through some of the darkest valleys and stood on some incredible mountaintops together. Nicole's strength, her heart, and her transformation inspire me every single day. She reminds me that redemption is real, and that none of us are beyond the reach of God's grace.

To all the friends who've stood by me through the chaos, the silence, the relapses, the rebounds, and the rebirth—I see you. There are too many of you to name, but you know who you are. Your loyalty didn't just carry me—it kept me alive. Whether it was a late-night check-in, a simple prayer, or just refusing to give up on me when I had given up on myself, your love became part of the rescue mission God was orchestrating. Please know— it hasn't gone unnoticed or unappreciated. I love each of you in your own unique and powerful way, and I carry your kindness with me every single day. Thank you for loving me at my worst and still believing in my best.

🗩 Reflection Prompt: What promises have you made in your pain that you couldn't keep? Where in your life are you still carrying shame—and what would it look like to lay it down? What parts of your past still haunt you, and how might God be calling you to use them as a testimony?

📖 Scripture: Lamentations 3:22–23 (KJV)"It is of the Lord's mercies that we are not consumed, because his compassions fail not. They are new every morning: great is thy faithfulness."

Chapter Eight

Getting clean is one thing. Staying clean? That's war. Not a loud, Hollywood kind of war—but a slow, daily battle against the lies in your head, the ghosts in your memory, and the shame that still whispers when things get quiet.

Teen Challenge didn't magically fix me. It broke me open. So, God could start building something real. But building is slow. And rebuilding trust? That's even slower.

I had burned bridges. With friends. With family. And especially with my son. I remember writing letters that never got sent. Practicing phone calls, I was too ashamed to make. Praying that maybe—just maybe—God could still reach his heart while I was still trying to reclaim mine. I wanted to call and say, "I'm different now." But all he'd ever heard was, "I promise," followed by silence. So, I stayed in the fight. Quietly. Faithfully. Day by day. Task by task. Prayer by prayer. Doing the work. Not just to earn back trust—but to become the kind of man who could be trusted.

There were moments of doubt. Days I felt like I'd never be enough. But God kept whispering, "You don't have to go back. Just go forward." And I did.

One obedience at a time. One temptation resisted. One truth spoken. One wound handed over to Jesus instead of another relapse. The longer I walked in the light, the more the darkness started losing its grip.

Some mornings, I woke up and just stared at the ceiling, wondering if I was still that same man—still haunted, still bound. But then I'd get up, put my feet on the floor, and choose again. Choose healing. Choose hope.

Choose to believe that I didn't have to stay a prisoner of who I used to be.

Because the truth is, staying clean isn't just about saying no to drugs—it's about saying yes to life. To responsibility. To showing up even when it's hard. Especially when it's hard. It's in the tension of wanting to run but choosing to stay that God starts doing His deepest work.

And then… a breakthrough I'll never forget. I got word that my son wanted to talk. Not because someone made him. Not because he had to. Because he wanted to. We talked. We laughed a little. We cried. And I didn't try to defend myself. I just told him the truth: That I loved him. That I failed him. And that I was finally letting God fix what I never could. That conversation didn't erase the past. But it opened the door to the future. And that was enough.

There's a kind of quiet joy that comes when your prayers start getting answered—not all at once, but in small, steady miracles. One conversation. One hug. One "I love you" that isn't forced. That's how God rebuilds what the enemy tried to destroy.

But just as healing was starting to settle in… I got hit with another kind of pain. My nephew was shot and killed. Gone. Just like that. A young life snuffed out by a bullet and a broken world. And suddenly, grief came roaring back through my heart like a wildfire. This time, it wasn't shame or addiction breaking me—it was loss. I didn't know how to process it. I cried. I raged. I sat alone in silence asking, "Why him?" But somewhere in the pain, God whispered again: "Let this shape you. Let this soften you. Let this call you deeper."

You never get over a loss like that. You carry it. You wake up some mornings and forget for a second, and then it crashes back down on you like a wave you didn't see coming. I kept thinking of his smile, his laugh, the way he used to look at life like it owed him something beautiful. And now, he was gone. Just a memory and a headline.

So, I did something that changed me forever…

I started going door to door. Not to preach. Not to beg. Just to connect. To serve. To love. I knocked on doors of strangers with nothing but a willing heart and the truth of what God had done for me. And somehow… that was enough. I heard stories from addicts, mothers, hurting kids, lonely men. I prayed in driveways. Wept on porches. Hugged people I'd never met. And every time I showed up… God showed up, too. That door-to-door ministry changed me. It gave me backbone. It gave me empathy. It gave me purpose. Because I wasn't just surviving anymore. I was becoming a vessel.

I met a man named Jorge one day—angry, stiff, arms crossed like the world owed him something. He told me, "I don't do the church thing." I told him, "Me neither. I do the Jesus thing." He didn't say anything, but a week later I saw him again—this time with tears in his eyes. He said, "Something you said stuck with me. I can't shake it." We prayed right there, outside a trailer with broken blinds and a busted porch light.

Moments like that taught me that evangelism isn't about knowing all the right verses—it's about showing up and loving people where they're at. It's about listening without judging. It's about letting your scars speak louder than your sermons.

And every knock, every conversation, every "God bless you"—it all helped shape the man I am today.

The guys at the center started looking to me more, too. As a leader. A big brother. A voice they could trust. Not because I had it all together. But because I didn't. Because I'd been there. And I wasn't afraid to go back into the dark to pull someone else into the light. I was becoming a man who could be counted on. Who could be trusted. Who could be present. Not just for strangers. For my son. For my family. For anyone who needed hope.

I started praying with more confidence. I started sharing not just the pain of my past—but the peace of my present. I stopped worrying about being perfect and focused instead on being available. Because that's all God really needs—a willing heart.

That's the long way back. Not flashy. Not easy. But sacred. Because when you walk it with Jesus, even the miles feel holy.

🗩 Reflection Prompt: What relationship in your life feels too broken to restore? What pain have you been through that God might be asking you to use to help someone else? Ask Him to show you where your healing becomes someone else's hope.

▭ Scripture: Joel 2:25 (KJV)"And I will restore to you the years that the locust hath eaten…"

Chapter Nine

Some people think the end of a program is the end of the story. But for me, finishing Teen Challenge was more like closing the first book in a series God's still writing.

I didn't graduate yet—not officially. That moment's coming soon. But I completed the program. Had my completion ceremony, stood in front of the brothers and staff and family who'd watched me fall, rise, and fight like hell to stay standing.

And I'll tell you what—it wasn't pride I felt. It was awe. Because I knew I didn't get here on my own.

I had come in court ordered. Bitter. Burned out. But I stayed because something changed in me. And the man who stood at that ceremony wasn't the same one who walked through the doors months ago. I was more than clean. I was clear. Clear about who I was. Clear about what I'd survived. Clear about the call that was rising up in me.

But just as I began to walk in that light…darkness came knocking again.

I got the call that my older nephew had overdosed. Gone. Another soul lost to the same battle I had barely escaped. A young man I loved. Someone who still had life left. Snatched by the same poison I'd danced with for years.

The grief was immediate. Sharp. Loud. Unrelenting. I wept harder than I had in years.

But this time, I didn't run. I didn't numb out. I didn't disappear. I felt it. I brought it to the altar. Dropped it in God's hands with nothing but groans and broken prayers.

I remember falling to my knees in the prayer room that night. The floor was cold. My face was soaked in tears. My fists were clenched so tight they hurt. I cried out with every ounce of strength I had left. And you know what? God didn't answer with thunder. He answered with presence. A calm that wrapped around me like a blanket. A stillness that said, "I've got you."

And something wild happened there in the middle of that heartbreak…I realized I was strong enough to stand in the storm now. Not because I was tough. But because I was anchored. God had built something in me through the fire. And now that fire had purpose.

That loss deepened the call. It made every interaction with the guys at Teen Challenge feel heavier. More urgent. More real. I wasn't just talking recovery anymore. I was speaking from the middle of my own grief. And somehow, that grief gave me a louder voice—and a softer heart.

I started checking in on the younger guys more. Sitting with them after chapel. Asking questions others might avoid. Noticing when someone was too quiet, too guarded, too close to the edge. Because I knew those signs. I had worn that mask. And if my pain could give me eyes to see someone else's, then it was worth it.

Sometimes I'd walk into the dorms late at night, and you could feel the heaviness in the room. The kind that doesn't speak, but screams. I'd sit down on the edge of a bunk and just be there. No agenda. No sermon. Just presence. Sometimes that's all someone needs—someone who doesn't flinch when they tell the truth. Someone who's not scared of the mess.

Completion ceremony came with tears and hugs and claps. But in my heart, I wasn't celebrating an end. I was acknowledging a beginning. Graduation is still ahead. But now, I'm walking toward it with clarity, not confusion. I know who I am. I know what I've come through. And I know what I'm called to do. Not just stay clean. Not just stay safe. But to stand. To lead. To love the broken back to life—just like God did for me.

I no longer walk like a man afraid of relapse. I walk like a man redeemed, on assignment. Not perfect, but intentional. Not flawless, but fearless. Because when you've lost enough, and grieved enough, and been rebuilt from nothing—you start to realize that the fire inside of you is stronger than the fire around you.

And I carry that fire everywhere I go now. Into my relationships. Into my work. Into my worship. It's a fire that doesn't destroy, but refines. It burns away the lies and leaves behind something solid—something real. This isn't the end of the journey. It's the moment I finally understand why I had to walk through all that fire in the first place.

And I can't talk about the fire without talking about that weekend in September of 2024—Man Camp. That trip changed everything for me. It wasn't just a getaway. It wasn't just bonding. It was holy ground. I walked into those woods still carrying pieces of my past, still unsure if I was really free. But something happened out there—something sacred. Surrounded by men who were hungry for God, vulnerable before Him, and chasing after purpose, I felt a release I hadn't known I needed. During one of those quiet, powerful moments by the fire, I finally let go of what I thought manhood looked like and embraced what God says it is. It was at Man Camp that I realized I wasn't just healing—I was becoming. Becoming the man, the father, the leader, the warrior that God had designed me to be all along. I left that mountain marked. Different. Forever changed. That weekend didn't just reignite the fire—it clarified the call.

But for all the healing and hope I found—there are still echoes I carry.

See, I didn't just come out of Teen Challenge with a certificate and a testimony.

I came out with ghosts. Faces I can't forget. Conversations that never got finished.

People I loved who didn't make it.

I still think about my nephew—his laugh, his eyes, the way he'd light up a room before the weight of addiction dimmed that light.
I think about the what-ifs.
What if I had reached him sooner?
What if I had prayed harder, called more, fought differently?
But the truth is… I couldn't save him.

And I still grieve that.

Some days, the grief sneaks up quiet. Other times, it hits like a freight train.
But even in the middle of that ache, I hear God whisper:
"His story is not wasted. And neither is yours."

That truth doesn't erase the pain—but it gives it purpose.

And if I'm honest, there's more than just grief.
There's regret too.

I'm haunted by the people I manipulated in my addiction.
The ones I smiled at while I lied to their face.
The ones I sold false promises to, just to make rent—or just to get high.

Some of them were kind. Vulnerable. Lonely.
They let me into their homes. They gave me their trust.
And I broke it—for a commission.

Sometimes I close my eyes and I see them—people I'll probably never get to apologize to.
I see their disappointment. Their confusion.
I see the way I used my God-given gifts for gain instead of grace.
And it wrecks me.

But you know what? That wreckage keeps me real.

It reminds me that I'm not better than the guys I mentor now—I'm just further down the road.

It keeps me humble. It keeps me hungry for righteousness.

It keeps me praying that somehow, the man I am now can redeem what the man I was once broke.

Because this calling—it's not just about staying clean.

It's about being available.

About being the man who will sit in the mess, cry with the hurting, and speak life where death has tried to settle in.

That's why when I walk through the dorms at night, I'm not just checking on guys—I'm interceding for them.

Asking God to break through the walls they've built.

To speak louder than the lies.

To give them what He gave me: a moment where grace won the fight.

Every prayer I whisper, every tear I catch, every late-night conversation in the hallway—it's all part of the mission now.

This is more than recovery. This is rescue work.

And yeah, I haven't officially graduated yet. That celebration's coming.

But the real victory? It's already happening.

Every time I say yes to love over fear.

Every time I choose truth over comfort.

Every time I stand in the fire with someone who's on the verge of giving up.

That's graduation in the kingdom.

Not a tassel or a stage—but a life poured out for others.

And I can't help but look back and wonder…

How many doors did I knock on that were never meant to open?

How many times did I beg for worth from strangers when the only door that mattered—the one to my own heart—was the one I kept locked shut?

But I thank God that He never stopped knocking.

Through the overdose.
Through the lies.
Through the years I lost chasing shadows.

He kept knocking.
And when I finally opened the door, He didn't just come in—He rebuilt the whole house.

Now I walk like a man who's been reborn in the rubble.
A man who's not afraid to revisit the pain if it means leading someone else out of it.

I've been through hell, but I didn't come out empty-handed.
I came out with fire.
Not the kind that destroys—but the kind that ignites.
The kind that says, "There's still hope. There's still time. There's still a door waiting to be opened."

And I'll keep knocking—this time, not for a sale…
But for a soul.

🗩 Reflection Prompt: What recent pain or loss has tested your faith? How has God sustained you through it—and what might He be preparing you for through that fire? Write it out. Don't be afraid to wrestle with it. There's purpose buried in the pain.

🖵 Scripture:2 Corinthians 4:8–9 (KJV)"We are troubled on every side, yet not distressed; we are perplexed, but not in despair; Persecuted, but not forsaken; cast down, but not destroyed."

Chapter Ten

I used to think finishing the program would be the final step—like a period at the end of a sentence. But when I stood at my completion ceremony, looking around at the men and mentors who had watched me fall, break, and rise again… I realized something: God wasn't done. He didn't just want to rescue me. He wanted to position me.

I hadn't walked the graduation stage yet—that's still coming. But I had completed the program, and I knew this wasn't just a "well done." It was a commissioning. A call to step back into the same place that broke me, this time as a man ready to help build others up. So, I said yes to the 6-month internship. I didn't know what it would hold—but I knew I was no longer a student learning how to stay sober…I was a servant learning how to lead.

And let me be real—this internship has been no joke. It's one thing to recover for yourself. It's a whole different thing to help someone else through their storm while you're still drying off from your own. But there's something powerful about that. Because I don't speak from a pulpit—I speak from wounds that are still healing. When I talk to the guys, it's not theory. It's me too. It's "I remember what that felt like." It's "I still feel that some days."

There are days I've sat on the edge of my bunk and questioned everything. Days I've wrestled with the weight of ministry, wondering if I was really cut out for this. And in those moments, God doesn't scold—He reminds. He reminds me of where He pulled me from. He reminds me of the men who didn't give up on me. He reminds me that leadership isn't about being perfect—it's about being willing.

Some mornings, I wake up tired. Some days, I feel the weight of the responsibility. And I'd be lying if I said the enemy doesn't still whisper in my ear, "Who do you think you are?" But every time I feel that…God reminds me who I am. Not who I was. Not who I could've been. Who I'm becoming .A leader. A brother. A mentor. A man of God who's not afraid to step into the mess with someone else because he's lived it.

The internship has taught me to be consistent. To lead by example. To speak up when it's uncomfortable. To check on guys when I'd rather check out. To pray for someone else when I'm the one who needs it. And through all of that—God's been preparing me for something even bigger: The new center. They're building it now—walls going up, visions taking shape. And I'm praying with everything in me that when those doors open…I'll be walking in as staff. Not because I need a title. But because I've found something I never had before—a purpose bigger than my pain. I want to give what was given to me. I want to be the kind of man I needed when I first walked through those doors. And I want these guys to know: Freedom is possible. And you don't have to walk it alone.

And just like that—I walked out free. Not just spiritually… but legally. Not just in my heart… but in the system that once had its foot on my neck. That's the kind of God we serve. He doesn't just set you free—He removes the labels. He says, "You're not what you did. You're who I say you are."

That moment shattered something in me—something I didn't realize I was still carrying. Guilt. Shame. That internal courtroom I kept walking into, trying to plead my case. But the Judge of all creation already rendered the verdict: Not guilty. Redeemed. Called. And now every time I look in the mirror, I don't see a man bound by old charges—I see a man released for Kingdom work.

And I'm not wasting that freedom. This summer, I'm starting school. Finishing my degree. Not because I need letters after my name—But because I need to finish what I started. Because I'm not the quitter I used to be. Because I'm building something now. A legacy. A future. A message that says, "It's never too late to rise."

I used to chase dope. Now I chase purpose. I used to run from responsibility. Now I run toward it.I used to think freedom meant doing whatever I wanted. Now I know true freedom is the power to do what God's called me to do—even when it's hard.

So, no—I haven't graduated yet.

But man, I'm already walking in a kind of favor I never knew existed. I see it in the way doors open that should have stayed closed. I hear it in the way people speak over my life now—not as a warning, but as a blessing. I feel it when I stand beside a broken brother, lay a hand on his shoulder, and speak life into dry bones because I've seen mine come alive.

There's something powerful about walking in purpose after walking through fire. Every scar becomes a testimony. Every tear becomes a seed. And everywhere I go now, I go as a carrier of hope. Not because I'm special—but because I'm surrendered. Because I said yes. Because I didn't quit when quitting felt easier.

I'm not just surviving anymore. I'm stewarding. I'm sowing into lives. I'm standing in gaps I used to fall through. I'm holding the line for men who haven't yet realized there's a different way. And I count it the greatest honor of my life.

And just recently, another door opened—a big one. I officially received my certification to be a Peer Recovery Support Specialist. That title means something powerful to me. It's not just paper—it's proof. Proof that God has turned my pain into purpose. That all the nights I didn't think I'd make it, all the mornings I woke up in regret, all the prayers I barely knew how to pray—they weren't wasted. Now I get to stand with others in their process and say, "I've been there. And by the grace of God, I came out the other side." This certification isn't the end. It's another key in my hand to unlock doors for others who feel trapped in the dark.

There are moments I catch myself mid-conversation, looking into the eyes of a man who reminds me of who I used to be—and I get chills. Not because I'm afraid of going back, but because I know how far God has brought me. Sometimes I'll share a story from my lowest point and watch that wall begin to crack in someone else. That's when I realize this is what all the pain was for. This is what the sleepless nights and cold jail cells and trembling detox mornings prepared me for—to sit in sacred spaces with hurting people and remind them: 'You're not done. God's not done.'

Sometimes I sit in silence after everyone's gone to bed. I think about my future, my grandson on the way, my son finding his own way, the legacy I get to build now with clean hands and a whole heart. I picture the new center open and thriving, a place not just for sobriety—but for resurrection. And I picture myself there, not as the broken man begging for mercy, but as a reborn man walking in mission.

But I'm walking in something even stronger than a diploma right now. I'm walking in favor. And this is just the beginning.

⬭ Reflection Prompt: What season are you in right now—waiting? Building? Walking into something new? Write out what you've completed...and what God might be preparing you for next.

☐ Scripture:1 Peter 5:10 (KJV)"But the God of all grace, who hath called us unto his eternal glory by Christ Jesus, after that ye have suffered a while, make you perfect, stablish, strengthen, settle you."

Chapter Eleven

If you would've told me a few years ago that I'd be planning to go back to school, I would've laughed in your face. Not because I didn't want it. But because I never thought I'd make it this far. There was a time I couldn't hold a job, couldn't stay clean, couldn't finish anything—not even a thought before my mind wandered back to the next high. I was a master at starting over... and a stranger to finishing strong.

But now? I'm different. Not perfect. Not polished. But changed. Focused. Rooted. And this time, I'm going back to finish what I started.

This summer, I start school. Not because someone told me to. Not because I have something to prove to the world. But because I made a promise to myself—and to the people watching me walk this thing out. I promised I wouldn't just get clean. I'd build something. Something lasting. Something I could hand down. A legacy.

Going back to school isn't just about academics. It's about redemption in action. It's showing up for the younger me who thought he wasn't smart enough. It's honoring the boy who never had stability, never had encouragement, and had to grow up thinking survival was more important than success. It's proving to my son that his father isn't all talk. That I don't just speak change—I live it. That he can be proud to carry my name. It's becoming the man my nephews needed. The man my family can count on. The man God knew was buried under all that pain and addiction—and refused to give up on.

There's something holy about returning to a place you once believed was out of reach. When I walk into that classroom, I won't be carrying just a backpack—I'll be carrying years of pain transformed into purpose. I'll sit at that desk with a mind that used to be fogged with meth and depression, now clear and disciplined. I'll take notes with hands that once shook from withdrawals, now steady with determination.

Will it be easy? Absolutely not. There will be days I'll doubt myself. Days I'll stare at a book and feel like I don't belong. Days I'll wrestle with lies from the enemy that say," You're too old." "You missed your chance." "You're not cut out for this." But I've learned how to answer those lies. I'll answer them with discipline. With showing up. With taking notes, finishing assignments, and walking into every class like I belong there— because I do. Because God brought me here.

This isn't just about a classroom. It's about showing that recovery isn't just about getting out of a ditch—it's about building a future once you've climbed out.

It's about healing your brain. Reclaiming your time. Firing up your potential. Believing that it's not too late to live on purpose.

Some people spend their whole lives waiting for the right time to change. But I'm not waiting anymore. This is my time. Not because it's convenient—But because it's God-ordained. He didn't bring me through the storm just to sit still. He brought me through so I could build something beautiful.

So, when I sit in that classroom this summer, I won't just be a student. I'll be a symbol. A story. A miracle in motion. Not because I'm smart enough. But because I'm surrendered enough. And God honors obedience more than brilliance.

Every page I read, every test I take, every goal I set—It's all part of the bigger picture. I'm not just chasing a degree. chasing legacy.

I'll be walking in with scars—but also with wisdom. With experience. With a testimony. And every time I'm tempted to quit, I'll remember: The same God who got me clean…The same God who dropped my charges…The same God who gave me a second chance…He's the One who called me to this.

And every hour I spend studying, every time I show up when I don't feel like it, every small victory in the classroom will be a defiant act of faith. Not just for me—but for everyone who's been told they're too far gone. For every addict who thought they lost too much. For every former inmate who still hears the echo of handcuffs when they try to dream. I'm walking back into that world—not with shame, but with authority. The authority that comes from surviving hell and still choosing to hope.

I think about all the people who believed in me when I didn't believe in myself. My mom, who prayed through the worst nights. My mentors at Teen Challenge who poured truth into me even when I fought it. The guys in the program who told me, "You got this," when I didn't feel like I did. I carry all of them with me. Their belief is fuel. Their faith in me is a mirror I now finally recognize.

And now, I want to be that for somebody else. I want to be the voice that reminds someone they're still in the running. I want to be the shoulder someone leans on when they feel like quitting. I want to be the example that says, 'Look, if God can do it for me—He can absolutely do it for you.

This next chapter isn't just for me—it's for the next wave of men behind me, still crawling through their wilderness. I want to walk so boldly in my calling that others feel safe enough to stand up in theirs. I want to reach back, grab a hand, and say, 'Let's go together. There's room for both of us on the other side of pain.' Because the truth is, healing isn't meant to be hoarded.

Freedom isn't meant to be framed on a wall and forgotten. It's meant to be shared. Lived out loud. Offered freely. I want to be a walking invitation to hope. I want people to look at my life and say, 'If God can use him, He can use me too.' Because this isn't about ego—it's about echo. Echoing the grace I've been given into the broken places around me. Echoing the mercy that met me in motel rooms, in jail cells, in treatment centers, and now walks with me into classrooms. Echoing the truth that freedom isn't just a moment—it's a mission. And He finishes what He starts.

💬 Reflection Prompt: Is there something you once walked away from that God might be calling you back to? What dream or goal has fear kept on pause in your life? Write it down. Speak life over it. Then take one step forward.

📖 Scripture: Ecclesiastes 7:8 (KJV)"Better is the end of a thing than the beginning thereof: and the patient in spirit is better than the proud in spirit."

Chapter Twelve

Of all the roles I thought I'd never reclaim…"Dad" was at the top of the list. There were years where that word felt like a ghost. A reminder of what I wasn't. A mirror I couldn't look into. I'd made promises to my son—so many promises. That I'd be there. That I'd stay clean. That I'd show up. And each time I fell back into the dope, those promises fell with me. I missed birthdays. I missed moments. I missed trust. And the guilt of that? It clung to me like a second skin.

But something happens when you start walking with God. He doesn't just clean your hands—He starts restoring your reach. Little by little, my relationship with my son started healing. Not overnight. Not without pain. with honesty. With effort. With consistency.

I didn't walk back into his life expecting praise. I came back willing to take the slow road. Willing to earn what I once took for granted. Willing to prove, through action, that I was no longer the man who disappeared. And slowly… something shifted. We started talking more. Laughing again. Sharing pieces of life, we'd both lost time on.

At first, every conversation felt like walking through a field of landmines. I didn't know what would trigger pain, what would bring up resentment, or what silence might mean. But I kept showing up. Not with perfect answers—but with real presence. I learned to listen more than I spoke. I learned to stop trying to defend the past and just focus on building a new present. One brick at a time.

And then came the news that stopped me in my tracks…My son is having a son.

I'm going to be a grandfather. And when I heard that…Something inside me broke and healed at the same time. Because I remember holding my boy as a baby, swearing I'd always be there. And now he's stepping into fatherhood—And I finally get the chance to be present for it.

This isn't just about legacy anymore. This is about restoration. God didn't just give me another chance for me—He gave me another chance to walk beside my son, and help him raise a new life without the shadows I once carried. This time, I'll be there for the early mornings. The milestones. The stories. The teaching moments. The chance to say, "I love you," and have it land—not feel like an apology.

I think about what it'll be like to hold my grandson. To trace his tiny fingers and feel the full weight of grace in my arms. To whisper prayers over him while he sleeps. To be a safe place for him—not just a provider of gifts, but a provider of presence. A man he can trust. A man he can run to. A man who broke the generational curse, not just for his father—but for him, too.

I used to worry I'd never get to fix what I broke. Now I understand—it's not about fixing. It's about showing up different. Being faithful. Being soft when needed. Strong when called for. And anchored in grace every step of the way.

I want my grandson to know the real me. Not the version the world judged. But the man who walked through fire to stand here clean. The man who cried out to God in silence. The man who never gave up—because love wouldn't let him.

I want to teach him how to fish. How to pray. How to fail and get back up again. I want to be there when he scores his first touchdown or loses his first tooth. I want him to grow up knowing the power of God because he saw it alive in me. And I want him to carry that same fire, that same faith, into a world that will try to steal both.

This is more than just becoming a father again. This is becoming the man I always hoped my son would see. And now, he does. And my grandson? He'll never have to question whether his grandpa is in his corner. Because I will be. With open arms. A clear mind. And a full heart.

I imagine one day sitting on the porch with my grandson, watching the sun dip below the horizon. I'll tell him stories—not just the victories, but the valleys. I want him to know that strength doesn't mean perfection. It means perseverance. It means you keep showing up even when it hurts. That real men cry, pray, forgive, and stay. That redemption isn't just something God gives—it's something we carry forward.

I think about how I want him to see the world—with eyes wide open, not jaded, but discerning. I want to pour into him the wisdom I paid for with pain. Teach him to love deeply, lead humbly, and listen carefully. I want to be the kind of grandfather who doesn't just hand down advice— but hands down a legacy of courage, compassion, and conviction.

I picture the day he'll ask me about my past—not with fear, but with curiosity. And I won't hide it. I'll tell him the truth. Not to glorify the darkness, but to magnify the grace. I'll tell him about the chains I broke by the power of God. About the nights I thought would be my last. About the prayers that pulled me from the brink. And I'll look him in the eyes and say, "Son, you come from a long line of fighters—but now, you come from freedom."

I want him to know that our story didn't end with pain—it turned a corner into promise. That with God, the curse doesn't get the final word—redemption does. And that whatever he faces, he won't face it alone. Because I'll be there. And more importantly, so will the God who raised me back up from the ashes.

But if I'm being real, there's still a part of me that grieves everything I missed. I think about all the birthdays that passed without me. The candles he blew out without his dad there to cheer him on. The photos I'm not in. The parties I skipped out on—not because I didn't care, but because I was too high, too ashamed, too lost in my own destruction. I remember the silence on the other end of the phone when I'd try to call. The hesitations in his voice. The disappointment in his eyes. Those memories haunt me sometimes—not to crush me, but to remind me of what grace has truly restored.

There were moments he needed me and I wasn't there. When bullies came. When school got hard. When life got confusing and a boy just needed his father. I abandoned my post. I left him exposed to a world that doesn't play fair. And that truth cuts deep. But it also fuels my mission now. I can't go back and relive those days, but I can make sure that moving forward—he and his son will never question where I stand. I'm done making promises. I'm making presence. I'm building trust, not with big declarations, but with daily decisions. One moment at a time.

I know there are other fathers out there reading this—sitting in jail cells, rehab dorms, or just in the quiet corners of guilt—thinking it's too late. Thinking they've lost their shot. Let me tell you something: if you're still breathing, it's not too late. Your child may be angry. They may be hurt. They may not believe your words anymore. But God can do what you can't. God can heal what you broke. You don't have to be perfect— you just have to be present. Start where you are. Show up. Stay consistent. And trust that what you water in humility, God will grow in grace.

Some days you'll feel like you're climbing uphill with nothing but regret in your backpack. But every step you take in the right direction counts. Every text. Every prayer. Every conversation where you just listen and don't defend yourself—that's healing. That's legacy. That's what turns broken bloodlines into testimonies of redemption.

💬 Reflection Prompt: Who in your life are you ready to show up for in a new way? Is there someone you've hurt or drifted from that God may be nudging you to pursue? Write a prayer for that relationship—and ask God to guide the restoration process.

📖 Scripture: Malachi 4:6 (KJV)"And he shall turn the heart of the fathers to the children, and the heart of the children to their fathers..."

Chapter Thirteen

I never used to dream about the future. When you're stuck in addiction, your world shrinks down to the next fix, the next lie, the next excuse. The future? That felt like fiction. Something other people talked about while I was just trying to survive the day.

But now? Now that I've come through the fire, carrying both scars and testimony—I can finally look forward. Not just with hope, but with clarity. With conviction. With purpose. I don't ask, "What if I never get out of this?" anymore. Now I ask, "What if God really uses all of this? "And He is.

Finishing the program and stepping into this internship has been more than a transition—it's been a confirmation. God didn't pull me out of the pit just to sit still. He pulled me out to raise me up. I was never meant to stay a student forever. I'm called to lead. To disciple. To mentor. To go back into the places where I was once lost and help pull someone else out.

That's why I said yes to the internship—and why I'm praying to become staff at the new Teen Challenge center that's being built. When those new doors open, I want to be standing there—not just with a title, but with a heart on fire. I want to be the first face a new guy sees when he walks in hopeless, skeptical, and broken. I want him to know he's not alone anymore. Because I remember what that walk felt like. I remember thinking I'd never belong. And I want to be the proof that not only can he belong—he can be rebuilt.

While God is rebuilding me, He's also restoring what I never thought I'd recover. All of my legal charges? Dropped. Gone. Erased. I used to think I'd always carry the label of "felon," "criminal," "addict." But God stepped into that courtroom with favor and said, "Not anymore." What the system meant for chains; He turned into freedom. He didn't just clean up my spirit—He cleared my name.

And with that freedom came fire. The kind of fire that keeps you up at night dreaming, planning, praying. The kind of fire that fuels vision even on days when doubt tries to sneak in. Because I know now—God doesn't just save you from something. He saves you for something.

That's why I'm not wasting this chance. This summer, I'm going back to school. Not because I want a title or need to prove anything to the world, but because I promised myself—and God—that I'd finish what I started. I'm going back to claim what I once threw away. I'm walking back into the classroom, not as a statistic, but as a symbol of restoration.

It won't be easy. There will be days when the work feels heavy, when the enemy whispers old lies. But I'm not that man anymore. The same God who got me clean will give me the strength to finish. Every class, every assignment, every late-night study session—it's all part of the new foundation I'm laying. Not just for me, but for the generations after me. For my son. For my grandson. For the men I haven't even met yet who need to see that it's never too late to rise.

Now when I close my eyes, I see more than just staying sober—I see a vision. I see men in recovery centers, classrooms, and churches, listening to someone who's lived it. I see recovery homes being built, outreach happening on the streets, books and devotionals written by a man who once couldn't finish anything. I see myself speaking to the ones who still think they're too far gone. And I see God using my voice to say, "You're not."

Sobriety is no longer the finish line. It's the launchpad. It's the bare minimum for what I know God is calling me to. I don't want to just be clean. I want to be powerful. I want to be present. I want to be consistent. I want to be a man who shows the world what grace looks like in action.

If I had the mic and the world was listening, I'd say this: Don't let shame silence your future. Don't let the years you lost convince you that your best ones are behind you. Don't let the lies you've believed make you forget who you were created to be. God still writes beautiful stories with broken pens. I'm living proof.

This chapter of my life is about dreaming again—and building what addiction tried to burn down. I'm not afraid to hope anymore. I'm not scared of purpose. I'm walking toward it, one step at a time. And I'm doing it with a fire that doesn't come from hype—it comes from healing.

The future is no longer a threat. It's an invitation. And I've already RSVP'd "yes."

Some days I walk the grounds at Teen Challenge and I just stop and look around. I think about the men who will fill the beds next month. Next year. Five years from now. Men who haven't hit bottom yet. Men who will walk through those doors thinking their life is over. And I get fired up thinking—I might be there to meet them. To speak life into them. To walk them through the fire like someone once did for me. Because it's not just about rebuilding myself. It's about raising up an army of men who know what it means to fall and get back up.

I don't just want to dream big—I want to help others dream again too. That's why I'll keep showing up. Keep serving. Keep sharing. Not from a place of arrival, but from a place of ongoing redemption. God opened doors I once thought were sealed shut forever. One of the biggest was stepping into the Resource & Development position here at the center. It wasn't just a job—it was a divine assignment. A way to start preparing, not just for a title, but for the purpose God planted in me. I'm not waiting until the new center opens to get ready—I'm already in motion. Already learning, already serving, already pouring myself into this mission with a heart that stays lit with holy fire. I want to walk through those new doors not just with credentials, but with character. With conviction. With credibility that comes from consistency and calling. Because I believe our future isn't just something we walk into—it's something we build. One act of obedience. One step of faith. One surrendered day at a time.

◯ Reflection Prompt: What dreams have you buried because you thought you missed your chance? What vision is God showing you now that you're finally free to see it? Write it down—big, bold, scary if it has to be. Then ask God to give you the strength to walk it out one step at a time.

☐ Scripture: Habakkuk 2:2–3 (KJV)"And the Lord answered me, and said, Write the vision, and make it plain upon tables, that he may run that readeth it. For the vision is yet for an appointed time... though it tarries, wait for it; because it will surely come, it will not tarry."

Chapter Fourteen

It's easy to talk about freedom when you're fresh off a breakthrough. When the tears are still wet, the applause still echoes, and grace feels like a wave that's just washed over your whole soul—freedom feels big, bold, undeniable.

But the real test of freedom? It's what you do on a Tuesday morning. It's how you respond when no one's watching. It's how you carry yourself when your phone's not ringing and your name's not being called. It's in the quiet, not the celebration. That's where I am now. Not just fighting to stay sober—but learning how to live free.

Every day, I wake up with choices. I can drift, or I can press in. I can coast, or I can climb. I can fall back into survival—or I can lean into abundance. Freedom isn't the absence of struggle. It's the presence of intentionality. So, I make my bed. I open the Word. I reach out to brothers who keep me anchored. I lead by example—even on the days I feel quiet or heavy or unseen. Not because I'm performing. But because discipline is now a form of worship.

Some days I still hear the old voices. You know the ones: "You'll mess this up." "This won't last." "Who do you think you are?" And on those days, I remind myself of who I've become.

A man who no longer listens to shame. A man who answers fear with faith. A man who shows up. Not perfectly. But consistently.

And here's the thing about consistency—it's quiet. It doesn't get applause. No one throws a party because you got out of bed and read your Bible. No one shouts amen because you told the truth or humbled yourself in a moment of tension. But heaven notices. Hell trembles. And the version of me that used to quit? He's silenced every time I choose the narrow road.

The beauty of this season is that God is showing me how to live from identity, not just activity. I'm not just the guy who does recovery things. I'm a son. A leader. A man of God. And I'm learning to enjoy this life. Not just survive it.I laugh more. I pay attention. I walk slower and breathe deeper. I find God in the ordinary—a hot cup of coffee, a clean kitchen, a conversation that heals instead of hides. I used to think freedom would be loud and dramatic. Turns out, it's peaceful. And that peace? It's priceless.

I'm also staying connected to purpose. Whether it's helping out at the center, taking initiative during my internship, or preparing for staff life, I don't take these moments for granted. Because I know what it feels like to wake up hopeless. And now? I wake up with vision. I'm building momentum, not just holding ground. And every day that I stay grounded, someone else out there gains hope. That's not pressure—it's privilege.

I've also learned the importance of rest. Real rest. Not numbing out, but soul rest. Time with God. Time in prayer. Time in quiet, not because I'm hiding—but because I'm healing. Rest used to feel like laziness. Now I know it's obedience. Because even warriors need to lay their swords down at night.

And I'm dreaming more. About school. About future ministry. About sharing this story from pulpits, podcasts, prisons—wherever God sends me. But I don't have to chase that. I just stay faithful where I am. Because when you're walking with God, the door you're called to will open when you're ready. Until then, I stay planted. Rooted. Focused. I'm not chasing hype—I'm building a harvest.

I've come a long way from the boy who begged for food, from the man who ran to meth to feel alive, from the ghost who let shame keep him silent. Now I'm fully here. Free. And becoming more myself every single day.

And maybe that's the greatest evidence of freedom—not that life is perfect, but that I no longer run from it. I don't escape into fantasy, substances, or chaos. I show up to my life with both hands open. I face the hard days with prayer instead of panic. I celebrate the good ones without fear of them slipping away. I forgive faster. I stay longer. I speak softer.

I'm learning how to love better, too. Not just the people who are easy to love—but the ones who mirror the old me. I see myself in them, and it keeps me humble. It keeps me praying. It keeps me reaching out to the guy in the back row, the one who doesn't believe in himself yet. Because I know what it's like to be him. And I know what's possible when someone believes in you anyway.

Freedom has also taught me to be grateful for the slow days. For the normal ones. For the days with no drama, no highs, no applause. Just a quiet soul and a clear mind. That's the kind of wealth I never knew I could have.

I don't take that for granted—not for a second. Because for years, I lived with chaos as my compass. I didn't know how to breathe unless something was breaking, bleeding, or burning. Peace felt like boredom. Stillness felt like punishment. But now I see—those quiet moments? They're sacred. They're holy. They're evidence that God has done a deep work, not just in my behavior, but in my wiring.

I'm finally learning how to live without drama. To rest without guilt. To feel joy without waiting for it to be ripped away. I've stopped bracing for the bottom to fall out—and started believing that I'm allowed to be blessed. Not because I've earned it. But because God delights in giving good gifts to His kids. And this life? This peace? This freedom? It's a gift I open every morning with gratitude in my gut and fire in my bones.

And that fire? It's not just for me. It's for the man still trapped in the cycle, the mother praying for her son to come home, the kid who's starting to believe the lie that he's too broken to matter. My freedom isn't private—it's a beacon. A light on a hill that says, "You can make it, too."

Because if God can take a shattered life like mine and shape it into something steady, hopeful, and whole—He can do it for anyone.

I walk with more purpose now, even in the little things. The way I talk. The way I serve. The way I pray before I speak. Because every part of my life is now a testimony. Not to my strength—but to His mercy. Not to my will—but to His Spirit. That's real freedom. It doesn't just change your habits—it changes your heart.

It changes your eyes too—how you see people, how you see pain, how you see purpose. These days, I walk into a room and I don't look for the spotlight—I look for the one sitting in the shadows. The man with his head down. The one fidgeting with shame in his hands. I used to be him. And now I get to tell him, 'You're not stuck. You're not beyond help. And no matter what you've done, you're not disqualified from grace.'

That's what freedom gives you—the courage to speak into places you once hid from. The compassion to be patient with people who are still learning how to heal. The strength to stand firm when temptation whispers and the humility to admit when you need help. Because freedom isn't the end of the journey—it's the start of one that actually matters.

It's a freedom that's meant to be multiplied. That's why I tell my story again and again—because I know there's someone out there who hasn't yet heard the sound of their own chains breaking. I want my life to be evidence that redemption is real, that God really does reach down into the dirt and pull people out of it—not just to clean them up, but to crown them with purpose.

Every breath I take is a reminder that I could have died in my addiction. But I didn't. I could've been another statistic, another sad ending. But I'm not. And that means I have a responsibility. To show up. To testify. To carry the light like it cost something—because it did. Jesus paid for it, and now I live to reflect it.

🗩 Reflection Prompt: What does "freedom" look like in your everyday life? Are there habits, thoughts, or relationships you still need to surrender in order to walk in that freedom fully? Journal it honestly. Your daily rhythm reflects your deepest beliefs.

☐ Scripture: Galatians 5:1 (KJV)"Stand fast therefore in the liberty wherewith Christ hath made us free, and be not entangled again with the yoke of bondage."

Chapter Fifteen

There was a time when I didn't care if I left anything behind.
I was just trying to get through the day.
Trying to get high enough not to feel.
Trying to disappear without making too much noise on the way out.

But now?
Now I think about legacy all the time.
Not in a prideful way—
But in the way a man does when he realizes he's still here for a reason.

God didn't bring me through everything He did just so I could be a good story.
He brought me through to build something bigger than myself.
I'm not just a survivor.
I'm a foundation layer.
I'm laying down something solid for those coming after me—
my son, my grandson, the men I mentor, and even the strangers I'll never meet whose chains might break just from hearing what God did in me.

This legacy? It's not made of money.
It's made of integrity.
Of presence.
Of truth-telling and faith-walking.
Of showing up when it's inconvenient and loving people when they don't know how to love themselves.

I want my son to know me not just as the man who turned it around…
But as the man who stayed the course.
The man who didn't just clean up but stepped up.

The man who stood firm, even when life hit again.

The man who could say "no" to the old life not because he had to, but because he finally understood his worth.

I want my grandson to grow up hearing stories about who I used to be—

but only so he can understand the power of who God is.

I want him to hear the truth—not sanitized, not sugarcoated.

I want him to know that his bloodline carries battle scars, but it also carries blessing.

That the same God who rescued me will walk with him, too.

I want him to know that addiction didn't win.

That generational curses can break.

That men can rise from the ashes and lead with love.

That his name carries weight now—because mine was redeemed.

Legacy is built in the little things now.

How I speak.

How I show up.

How I stay consistent when no one's clapping.

It's built in keeping my word.

In calling someone back when I say I will.

In praying when I'd rather scroll.

In listening when someone's hurting instead of trying to fix them.

It's built in how I walk past temptation and whisper, "Not today. I've come too far."

It's built in how I take everything the enemy meant to use to destroy me, and I turn it into fuel to reach someone else.

I've started thinking more about the end of my life—not in a morbid way, but in a focused way.

When it's all said and done, I don't want to be remembered for my past.

I want to be remembered for what I built after the pain.

I want people to say,

"He didn't give up."

"He told the truth."
"He helped people heal."
And I want my family to say,
"He loved us hard. He stayed when it got hard. And he finished strong."

This legacy?
It's sacred.
It's why I stay close to God.
Why I stay honest about the temptations.
Why I don't pretend I've got it all figured out.
Why I keep my recovery close, not hidden.
Because if I let pride sneak in, I'll forget the pit I came from.
And if I forget the pit, I risk slipping back into it.

Legacy isn't just about building something to leave behind.
It's about living in a way that leaves no doubt about who carried you through.
It's about living like someone's watching—not out of fear, but out of awareness that your steps might be guiding someone else's.
It's about choosing humility over hype, faithfulness over flash, and obedience over applause.

The world sees change as success.
But real legacy?
That's when your transformation becomes someone else's foundation.
That's when your healing becomes a blueprint.
That's when your story becomes someone else's survival guide.

That's what I'm chasing now.
And by the grace of God,
that's what I'm leaving behind.

I think about the people who helped shape me—the ones who believed in me when I didn't believe in myself. Some of them probably didn't even realize the impact they had, but their presence, their words, their example left fingerprints on my soul. That's the kind of legacy I want to leave. Not fame. Not attention. Just impact. Quiet, steady, eternal impact.

I want to live in such a way that my grandson's children will one day hear about a man named Brent who refused to quit. Who walked with a limp but kept walking. Who told the truth even when it hurt. Who lived out the Gospel not just in words but in action. Who loved hard, served faithfully, and always pointed to the One who made it all possible.

And if God grants me more time, I'll keep planting seeds I may never see bloom. Because legacy isn't always something you get to witness—it's something you build in faith, believing that long after you're gone, the light you carried will still shine in someone else's story.

Sometimes I wonder how many lives we impact without ever knowing it. A kind word, a prayer whispered for a stranger, a moment of encouragement dropped into someone else's storm—those are legacy moments too. Not everything we leave behind will have our name on it, but that doesn't make it any less eternal.

Legacy isn't measured in grand gestures, it's measured in consistency. In faithfulness. In the way you keep choosing light even when the night is long. It's in the apologies that heal wounds. In the forgiveness that stops a cycle. It's when someone says, "Because of you, I didn't give up." That's the kind of legacy I want. Not headlines—but healing.

And I pray that when people remember me, they don't remember a man who was perfect, but a man who was persistent. A man who got back up. A man who clung to Jesus when nothing made sense. A man who left behind more than memories—he left behind a model.

I want the men who cross my path to feel that same spark—that same hope I once thought was lost forever. I want them to walk away not thinking how strong I was, but how strong God is. Because legacy isn't built by willpower—it's built by surrender. It's built when a man finally lays down his pride and lets God rewrite his future. That's what I've done, and that's what I'll keep doing, every day He gives me breath.

I carry that calling with a quiet urgency. Not a panic—but a purpose. I'm not rushing to the finish line, but I'm not wasting a single step either. Every prayer I whisper, every conversation I lean into, every act of obedience—it's all bricks in the foundation I'm laying. Not for my glory. For His.

And when I meet Him face to face one day, I want to be able to say, "Lord, I spent it all. Every gift You gave, I used. Every scar You healed, I showed. Every day You gave me, I gave back.

Because that's what legacy ultimately is—a life poured out. Not hoarded, not hidden, but given. Given to the ones coming behind you, to the ones struggling beside you, and even to the ones who may never know your name but will walk on the path your life helped clear.

I may not leave behind buildings or bank accounts, but I will leave behind a legacy of breakthrough. Of bold prayers. Of second chances that turned into sacred callings. I want to be remembered as a man who didn't just talk about faith—but lived it loud and real and messy and brave.

And maybe one day, long after I'm gone, someone will open this book, feel the Spirit stir in their chest, and say, "If God could do that for him… He can do it for me too."

That right there? That's a legacy worth everything."

And if you're reading this right now, wondering if it's too late for you to build something beautiful—let me say this with all the fire in my chest: It's not. You are not too far gone. Your story isn't over. The same God who resurrected my life can rewrite yours. Brick by brick. Day by day. Don't wait until you feel ready. Legacy starts the moment you decide to live differently. It starts with one surrendered 'yes.' One prayer whispered through the tears. One act of courage when you feel weakest.

Maybe your legacy won't look like mine. That's okay. It's not supposed to. Your legacy will carry your fingerprints—your voice, your tears, your victories. Let it be honest. Let it be holy. Let it be built in the trenches, not the spotlight. Because that's where real things grow.

So take today. Lay the first stone. Speak the first truth. Forgive the first wrong. And trust that every step you take toward God is a step into the legacy He's already planned for you.

Legacy also means facing your past with courage so it doesn't steal from your future. That's a part of this journey too—making peace with the younger version of myself who didn't know how to cope, how to love, how to live. I still think about that version of me. Sometimes I look in the mirror and whisper, "You're safe now. You made it." That boy in me still heals a little more every time I show up with integrity, with intention, with grace.

And it's not just about the men I mentor or the family I hope to influence. It's about the stranger scrolling late at night, numb and tired, who stumbles across a testimony and sees their own story in my scars. Legacy is digital now too. These words I'm writing might outlive me. They might echo in a prison cell, a rehab dorm, or a quiet bedroom where someone's praying their first desperate prayer in years. That matters.

The legacy I'm building is not about being remembered. It's about making sure God is. It's about helping the hopeless remember that grace still finds us. That healing is still real. That joy can exist even after devastation.

So I'll keep writing. I'll keep speaking. I'll keep walking this out. Because it's not just about where I've been. It's about who's watching me walk now, and who's starting to believe they can walk too.

💬 Reflection Prompt:
What kind of legacy are you building right now—by your actions, your habits, your words?

If your life ended today, what would people say you stood for?

Write out the kind of legacy you want to leave. Then take one small action today that aligns with it.

⬚ Scripture:
Proverbs 13:22 (KJV)
A good man leaveth an inheritance to his children's children:
and the wealth of the sinner is laid up for the just.

Chapter Sixteen

There's a prayer I've been praying quietly for a while now.
It's not fancy.
It doesn't come with big words or churchy phrases.
It's simple. Honest. From the gut.
"Use me, Lord."

Not just because I'm clean.
Not just because I've come through the storm.
But because I know what it's like to be desperate, to feel worthless, to believe the lie that it's too late.
And now I know the truth—
God doesn't just save us to save us.
He saves us to send us.

I don't want to just stay sober.
I want to be a vessel.
I want to walk into rooms where shame lives and bring light with me.
I want to speak to the addict still stuck, the father who walked away, the man drowning in regret—and let them know:
"You're not beyond God's reach."

I want my life to shout what my voice sometimes can't:
"There's still hope."

I'm not trying to be a pastor.
I'm not chasing a microphone.
But if God opens a door for me to speak—to share what He's done— I'll walk through it every single time.
Because I don't need a stage to minister.
I've got a story.

And I carry it like a weapon.
Not against people—but against darkness.

Because the devil tried to kill me.
Tried to keep me addicted, angry, ashamed.
Tried to convince me that I was too far gone.
But God said,
"Watch what I can do with a surrendered life."

Now when I pray, I don't just ask for strength.
I ask for opportunity.
Lord, send me to the hurting.
To the jail cells.
To the treatment centers.
To the streets.
To the places I used to run from.
To the men still trying to fill the hole in their chest with smoke and silence and self-hate.

Because I know how to speak their language.
Not because I studied it.
But because I lived it.

I remember what it feels like to sit in a circle of chairs and lie through your teeth because honesty hurts too much. I remember what it's like to sleep with one eye open in a halfway house, wondering if you'll make it through the night without relapsing. I remember hitting my knees in a motel room, high out of my mind, begging God to either kill me or save me—because I couldn't take another day of surviving.

That memory fuels my mission.
It reminds me that I'm not just a man with a testimony—I'm a man on assignment.

My heart burns for the ones who sit in chapel but haven't let the Word touch their soul yet.

For the men who say they want freedom but are still afraid of what healing will expose.

For the dads who think it's too late to get their kids back.

For the sons who think their fathers will never change.

I carry them in my prayers.

In my silence.

In my steps.

Because I know what it feels like to be them.

And I know what it feels like to be found.

God, use me.

Use my past.

Use my pain.

Use my scars.

Use the chapters I once tried to rip out of my story.

I don't need to be polished.

Just present.

Just available.

Just willing.

The world needs more real.

More honesty.

More stories that sound like mine—raw, broken, but dripping with redemption.

That's what I want to offer.

Not just recovery.

Revival.

One man at a time.

So, I'll keep showing up.

I'll keep writing.

Keep speaking.

Keep leading.

And I'll keep praying that every piece of pain I walked through will become purpose in someone else's healing.

Because that's what grace does.
It doesn't just clean you up.
It sends you out.
And I'm ready, Lord.
I'm ready.

But being ready doesn't mean I've arrived. It means I've learned how to walk forward while still bleeding sometimes. It means I've learned to pray when I don't have words, to lead even when I feel unqualified, and to trust God's hand when I can't trace it. I've learned that ministry isn't about perfection—it's about proximity. Being close enough to the broken to feel their pain, and close enough to the Spirit to carry healing.

I still feel the weight of my past some days. Not like chains, but like a mantle. A reminder. A calling. Every scar I carry whispers, "This is who you were. But this is who God is." That tension? It's sacred. It keeps me from forgetting. And it keeps me from faking it.

So I'll walk into the shadows others are too scared to face. I'll kneel beside the broken without flinching. I'll put my arm around the relapser, the prodigal, the skeptic, and say, "Me too. But look what God can do." Because I don't want a ministry built on a platform—I want one built on presence. On walking slow through the crowd. On making eye contact with the hurting. On sitting with someone long enough that they finally believe they're not alone.

I want to walk with the ones who don't know how to cry yet. Who've stuffed it down for so long they think emotion is weakness. I've been there. I know what it's like to look tough on the outside while falling apart inside. But I also know the healing that comes when you finally let the floodgates open and realize that tears aren't failure—they're freedom.

There's a sacred kind of strength in vulnerability. In being the one who says, "I don't have all the answers, but I'm still here. I'm still standing." That's the kind of leader I want to be. Not unreachable. Not untouchable. But real. Available. Flawed and faithful.

Because the ones who are hurting the most aren't looking for someone to preach at them—they're looking for someone who will sit beside them, listen without fixing, love without judging, and remind them that even in the dark, they're still worth something. That's the ministry God has trusted me with. And I will carry it like fire in my bones.

And if I'm honest, sometimes the weight of that fire scares me. Because I know what it cost me to carry it. I know how many nights I spent in silence, feeling forgotten. I know how many times I almost gave up—on life, on God, on myself. But I also know now that everything I went through wasn't wasted. Every detour, every heartbreak, every consequence—it was all groundwork for the calling I now carry.

I walk differently now—not because I'm perfect, but because I'm aware. Aware of the responsibility. Aware of the eyes watching. Aware that the same God who pulled me from the wreckage is now asking me to go back in and pull others out. And I won't take that lightly.

So when I kneel down in prayer, it's not just for me anymore. It's for the man still strung out in his car, crying and shaking. It's for the kid in juvenile detention wondering if he matters. It's for the tired mother praying for her prodigal son. It's for the ones who feel like statistics instead of souls. And it's for the future me, the one still becoming, still learning how to walk this out with boldness and grace.

I don't want applause. I want anointing. I don't need recognition. I need reach. I want to leave fingerprints on hearts, not just impressions on platforms. I want heaven to know my name—not because I shouted, but because I served.

If God gives me a stage, I'll use it. But if all He gives me is a folding chair in the back of a broken room, I'll take that too. Because the Gospel doesn't need spotlights—it just needs hearts willing to be lit on fire. If I can spark hope in just one person, then I've done my job. If one man lays down his pipe because my story gave him courage, then all the suffering was worth it.

I've come to realize that purpose isn't found in crowds—it's found in obedience. In small, sacred acts of faithfulness. In choosing to show up for the people God puts in front of me. Sometimes that's a stranger on the street. Sometimes it's a brother in the program. Sometimes it's my own reflection in the mirror, needing a reminder that I'm still called, still chosen, still redeemed.

And when the day comes that I'm called home, I don't want to leave behind questions about who I was or what I stood for. I want it to be unmistakable. I want people to say, "He lived on fire for Jesus. He didn't flinch. He didn't fake it. He gave God his everything, even when it cost him everything."

I want to be remembered not for how many people followed me, but for how many people I followed back into the dark until they could see the light for themselves. For how many men I stood beside in their lowest hour, not judging them, not fixing them—just being there, present, steady, willing. That's the work that lasts. That's the legacy that lives.

Because ministry isn't a position—it's posture. It's the posture of a heart that says, "I'll go." It's the posture of a man who doesn't wait until he's ready, but trusts God enough to move anyway. It's the kind of posture that bows low to wash feet, but stands tall when it's time to defend the weak.

And if there's still more fire in my bones, still more chapters to be written, then I'll keep saying yes. Yes to the pain that shaped me. Yes to the people I'm called to. Yes to the God who never stopped calling. Because that yes? It's where revival begins.

And revival doesn't always look like a packed church or a viral sermon. Sometimes it looks like one-on-one discipleship. Sometimes it looks like driving across town to visit someone who's hurting. Sometimes it looks like picking up the phone at midnight to talk a brother off the ledge. Revival can show up in tears at a coffee table, in whispered prayers on a back porch, or in the simple act of sitting quietly with someone who doesn't have the strength to say what they need.

It's in those moments—those small, holy, overlooked moments—that I feel closest to Jesus. Because He wasn't afraid to walk the long way for the one. He didn't overlook the outcast, the broken, the ignored. And I don't want to either. I want my life to be a series of "long walks" toward the ones everyone else gave up on. Because I was that man once. And someone walked toward me.

So let my feet stay dirty from the journey. Let my heart stay soft from the tears. Let my hands stay calloused from service. If that's the cost of being used—of carrying the Gospel into the corners—I'll pay it daily. With joy. With humility. With fire in my bones and the Word in my mouth.

Because I'm not done yet. Not even close.

💬 Reflection Prompt:
If God said "yes" to your wildest prayer to be used—what would that look like?
What spaces, people, or communities do you feel called to?
Write it out like a vision. Speak it into the atmosphere.

📖 Scripture:
Isaiah 6:8 (KJV)
Also I heard the voice of the Lord, saying, whom shall I send, and who will go for us? Then said I, here am I; send me.

Chapter Seventeen

If you would've told the old me that one day I'd wake up and be grateful for a quiet morning, a hot coffee, and a clean conscience—I would've laughed in your face.

Back then, my life thrived on chaos.
If it wasn't loud, dramatic, or destructive, I didn't know how to live in it.
Stillness felt like suffocation.
Peace felt like punishment.

But now?
Now I understand something I never used to believe:
Boring is beautiful.

There's a quiet kind of joy that comes from waking up with no shame.
From knowing you didn't lie to anyone yesterday.
From remembering everything you said and did—not through a fog of regret, but through clarity.

I used to chase a high.
Now I chase consistency.
And the more I've walked this out, the more I've realized:
Stability isn't weakness. It's warfare.
Because when you've lived most of your life in survival mode, choosing peace is actually one of the boldest things you can do.

These days, I find God in simple things.
A clean kitchen.
A good meal.

A hug from someone who knows my whole story but chooses to love anyway.

A long conversation with a brother in recovery who says, "Man, if you can do it, maybe I can too."

That's sacred to me now.

No flashing lights. No hype. Just purpose in motion.

I still get tempted.

The enemy doesn't pack up and leave just because you completed a program.

But now I know how to fight differently.

I don't swing wildly.

I don't run and hide.

I stand still, breathe deep, and remember everything God has already carried me through.

Temptation used to feel like a trap.

Now it feels like a test I'm finally equipped to pass.

And every time I say no to the old life, I say yes to everything I've built since walking away from it.

There's a phrase I keep close these days:

"Don't despise small things."

Because small things stack up.

Small choices build big integrity.

Small moments build strong legacies.

And it's the little stuff that people remember most.

The way you treated them.

The way you stayed consistent.

The way you loved without needing recognition.

That's the stuff that lasts.

I used to crave fireworks.

Now I crave faithfulness.

I used to be addicted to the rollercoaster.

Now I'm learning to love the daily climb—slow, steady, sacred.

There's no adrenaline rush in brushing your teeth, clocking in on time, keeping a promise, or eating a meal with your family.

But there's freedom in it.
And that freedom?
It's priceless.

I'm not done growing.
I'm not above falling.
But I'm walking now with my eyes wide open.
Not anxious. Not ashamed.
Just awake.
And the more I embrace the quiet, the more I hear God clearly.
He's not shouting. He's whispering in the stillness:
"Keep going. I'm proud of you. This is what legacy looks like."

I'm not bored.
I'm blessed.
And I'll never mistake peace for emptiness again.
Because what I used to call boring…
is exactly what I prayed for.

I used to think I needed to feel on edge to feel alive. That unless I was barely making it, I wasn't really living. But peace isn't passive. Peace is power under control. It's choosing stillness when your past tells you to panic. It's making your bed in the morning not because it matters to anyone else, but because it shows you're claiming this day—sober, grounded, and free.

Sometimes, I sit with my coffee and just breathe. No TV. No phone. No background noise. Just me and God. And in those moments, I remember the chaos I came from. The motel rooms. The drug runs. The lies. The self-hate. And I realize how far He's brought me.

Freedom isn't just escaping chains.
It's learning to live in the quiet without needing noise to distract you from your soul.

I find myself praying differently now.
Not always with long lists or desperate pleas.

Sometimes it's just, "Thank You, God, for this normal day."
Because normal used to be out of reach.
And now it's my miracle.

And let me be real—there are still days when I miss the thrill. Not the consequences, not the chaos, but that adrenaline rush that used to drown out my inner emptiness. It takes time to retrain a heart that was wired to survive firestorms to find beauty in a gentle breeze. But I'm getting there.

These days, my victories look different. They're quieter. More humble. Like saying no to an old trigger without anyone knowing. Like driving past a gas station that used to be my go-to spot for bad decisions—and not even flinching. Like choosing to go to bed early because I have purpose to wake up for.

I've come to believe that there's a holy rhythm to healing. It's not dramatic. It doesn't shout. It just keeps showing up. And if you're not careful, you might miss the miracle because you're too busy looking for the mountaintop moment, when the real growth was happening in the grind.

God's been teaching me that maturity looks like faithfulness in the unseen. It's how you behave when no one's clapping. How you respond when no one's watching. It's the slow work of rebuilding trust, character, and self-respect.

And it's beautiful.

There was a time I couldn't trust myself with stillness. If things got quiet, the memories got loud. The guilt would creep in like a fog, and I'd reach for anything to silence it—meth, manipulation, madness. I thought I needed the noise to survive. But what I really needed was permission to heal.

Now, when the world quiets down and the sun starts slipping behind the trees, I don't panic. I pause. I breathe. I listen for the voice that used to feel so distant. And I hear it more clearly now than ever before: "You're safe now."

Safe doesn't mean there's no struggle.
Safe means I'm no longer running.
I'm rooted.
Rooted in grace.
Rooted in truth.
Rooted in a peace I never thought I'd find in this lifetime.

Peace doesn't eliminate the past.
It reframes it.
It tells the story through God's eyes instead of mine.
Where I used to see failure, He shows me faithfulness.
Where I used to see waste, He shows me preparation.
Where I used to see ashes, He reveals beauty.

This is what restoration looks like—not flashy, not fast, but full.
And finally, I feel full.
Not from attention.
Not from applause.

But from the quiet, powerful presence of God holding all my broken pieces in His hands—and making something whole from them.

And in that wholeness, I've learned to stop apologizing for my peace. I don't have to explain why I guard my rest, why I cherish my routines, why I no longer answer chaos when it comes knocking. That's not fear—it's wisdom. That's not weakness—it's warfare.

I fought to get here.
I bled to get here.

And now that I've tasted real peace, I won't let go of it for anything. Not for validation. Not for toxic people. Not for old patterns that once felt like home. If it costs me my stability, my sobriety, or my sanity—it's too expensive.

I used to settle for anything that made me feel alive.

Now I seek only what helps me stay whole.

Because I've learned that God isn't just in the big breakthroughs—He's in the gentle routines, the sacred silence, the morning mercies that show up like clockwork.

This is peace. This is progress. This is proof that you can be healed and still humble, growing and still grounded. And this—this quiet life that I once thought was boring—is where I've found my greatest joy.

Some days I still wrestle with the quiet. Healing doesn't mean the old thoughts never come knocking—it just means I don't have to let them in anymore. I've learned how to let the peace of God guard my heart and my mind, even when the old scripts try to run their play. I speak truth now. I remind myself who I am. Whose I am.

I am not a slave to my past.

I am not the chaos I once called normal.

I am a man made new.

And part of that newness is learning to rest in rhythms instead of racing through life. I used to feel like I was always behind, always running, always trying to prove something. Now I realize—when you're walking with God, you're always right on time. He doesn't rush. He doesn't panic. And if I'm following His lead, I don't have to either.

So I keep showing up to the small things. Because they're not small to Him. They're seeds. And what I water today with obedience, I'll reap tomorrow in peace, in purpose, and in legacy.

And that legacy won't be built by accident. It's forged in the quiet choices I make every day—when no one's looking, when it'd be easier to coast, when I could justify cutting corners. But I don't. Because peace has become more valuable than the applause of others. Integrity has become my currency.

I used to think I needed to be extraordinary to matter. But now I know the most powerful lives are often the most consistent ones. The dads who come home every night. The men who stay when it's easier to run. The ones who keep showing up when there's no fanfare, no recognition, just a deep, steady yes to God.

So I'll keep walking.
Through quiet days.
Through simple routines.
Through a life that might look small to some—
but to me?
It's sacred ground.

This life of peace, of purpose, of faithful stability—it's not boring.
It's everything I never knew I needed.
It's the soil where legacy grows.
It's where I've finally learned to breathe.
It's where I've finally learned to live.

I used to think that testimonies only came from moments of rock-bottom and resurrection. But some of the most powerful testimonies I carry now are in the consistency—the Monday mornings when I show up early, the evenings when I choose prayer over scrolling, the days I serve without being seen. That's the miracle. Not just that I got free, but that I stayed free. That I'm choosing to walk it out one humble step at a time.

And I know now that this kind of peace wasn't given to me just to keep for myself. It's meant to be shared. Modeled. Offered to the ones who are still living in survival mode, convinced that chaos is the only way to breathe. I want them to see me and think, "If he found peace, maybe I can too."

Because this isn't just about staying clean. It's about building a life that makes freedom look possible. Tangible. Desirable. It's about showing that you don't have to live for the next high—you can live for the next holy moment, the next small act of faith, the next quiet sunrise with a heart finally at rest.

So I'll keep walking this road, one quiet miracle at a time. And I'll keep thanking God for boring blessings that turned out to be the very things that saved my life.

And if I could offer just one word to the man I used to be—the one still clawing through chaos for a breath of meaning—I'd say this: Keep going. The quiet is coming. And it won't feel like a cage anymore. It'll feel like coming home.

Because freedom isn't just the absence of chains. It's the presence of peace. It's the ability to sit still without fear. To love gently. To breathe deeply. To laugh without regret. To wake up and know you're exactly where you're supposed to be.

These are the miracles we often overlook—the ones wrapped in routine, clothed in ordinary, hidden in habit. But they're holy. And they are what rebuild a life.

So today, I'll thank God again for the slow days. For the boring blessings. For the silent mornings where healing hums instead of shouts. Because what I have now isn't loud, but it's lasting. It's not showy, but it's sacred.

And maybe that's the final proof that I've been changed:
I no longer need fireworks to know that God is near.
I just need breath in my lungs, peace in my spirit, and the steady whisper that says, "Well done. Keep going."

💬 Reflection Prompt:
Have you confused peace with boredom?
Where in your life do you need to stop chasing intensity and start cherishing stability?
Write about what "boring blessings" God has placed in your life lately.

📖 Scripture:

Zechariah 4:10 (KJV)
For who hath despised the day of small things?

Chapter Eighteen

It's a strange thing—to look back and not feel crushed by it.

There were years I couldn't even think about my past without feeling sick.

The memories came like a flood of shame, dragging me under.

The decisions I made. The people I hurt. The time I lost.

It all used to scream at me every time I tried to be still.

But now?

Now I can look back—and not flinch.

Because I know I'm not that man anymore.

Don't get me wrong—the pain is still there.

The loss still matters.

The damage I did to others, and to myself… I'll never pretend it didn't happen.

But I don't live there anymore.

I visit it sometimes, sure.

I let it remind me how far God has brought me.

But I don't unpack my bags there.

Because that man—

The one who got high to forget, who ran from his son, who sat in silence begging for a way out—

That man may have made a mess…

But he also survived.

He survived the children's home.

He survived the addiction.

He survived the heartbreak.

He survived himself.

And that survival?
That's something I honor now.
I'm not ashamed of him anymore.
Because that version of me—he walked through hell so I could stand here in freedom.

He endured so I could testify.
He failed so I could learn.
He broke so I could rebuild.

If I could talk to him now, I wouldn't scold him.
I'd thank him.
I'd look that old me in the eyes and say:
"You didn't quit. You wanted to, more than once. But you didn't.
And because of that, look where we are now."

That's what recovery gives you—
Not just clean time, but clear eyes.
You start to see the pain differently.
You start to see the purpose behind it.
You start to love the man you used to hate—because without him, you wouldn't be here.

There's a freedom that comes when you stop trying to erase your past...
And start owning it.
Not glorifying it.
Not hiding it.
Just telling the truth.

Because truth is the doorway to healing.
And when I tell my story now, I tell it with my head high.
Not because I'm proud of the chaos I caused—
But because I'm proud of the grace that caught me.

I can talk about my relapses.
My regrets.

My ruined moments.

My lost years.

And I can still smile at the end of the sentence.

Because I know how the story turns out.

God used it all.

Every high. Every tear. Every court date. Every conversation I avoided.

He used it all to break me down just enough for me to finally say, "I need You."

Looking back now, I don't feel regret.

I feel reverence.

Because I see the fingerprints of God all over my darkest chapters.

He didn't write the pain—but He sure knew how to edit the ending.

So here I am.

Looking back, not to dwell—

But to give thanks.

I thank God for the breakdowns, because they led to the breakthrough.

For the jail cells, because they became altars.

For the sleepless nights, because they birthed a desperation that reached heaven.

For every no I told Him that turned into a surrendered yes.

There was a time I hated my story. I wanted to bury it, erase it, rewrite it.

Now I want to shout it.

Because there's someone out there who's still stuck in chapter one, thinking that's the end.

But I'm living proof—you can turn the page.

You can be the cautionary tale and the redemption story.

The same mouth that once cursed God can learn to praise Him.

The same hands that once held poison can now hold purpose.

The same man who once ran from responsibility can now walk in legacy.

I don't carry shame anymore.
I carry wisdom.
I carry testimony.
I carry light into places I used to hide in.
And that, my friend, is what grace looks like in motion.

But even as I walk forward in healing, there are losses I carry with me—not as chains, but as fire.

One of those fires is the death of my nephew.
He died from what they called a drug overdose.
But deep down, I've never believed that was the whole truth.

Something about it never sat right. Too many unanswered questions. Too many inconsistencies. And in my heart—I know there's more to that story.

His life was not a statistic. He was not just another name in the system.
He was loved. He was funny. He had dreams. He had people who believed in him.
And even though his voice was silenced too soon, his story isn't over.
Because I still carry it.
His mother still carries it.
We are his voice now—and we will never be silent.

I refuse to let his memory fade into a file folder or a cold case.
Justice will come. Maybe not on our timeline. Maybe not in the way we want.
But I know this: God sees. God knows. And nothing done in darkness stays hidden forever.

Every time I speak, I carry his story with me.
Every time I minister to another hurting family, I think of him.

Every time I see someone barely hanging on, I fight a little harder—because I couldn't save him, but maybe I can help someone else live.

His death wasn't in vain.
It ignited something in me I didn't know I had—a holy rage against injustice, and a heart that will not rest until truth rises up from the ashes.

So as long as I breathe, I will speak his name.
And I will stand with his mother.
And we will carry his legacy.
Because his life mattered.
And no one—no system, no cover-up, no silence—can take that away.

And there's more pain I carry—another name I'll never stop saying.

My other nephew was only sixteen when he was shot and killed.
Sixteen.
Barely a man. Still just a boy.
With dreams in his chest and light in his eyes.

His life was cut short by a bullet, but the damage that bullet caused ripples through our family every single day.

I will always be his voice too.
He didn't get the chance to grow up.
Didn't get the chance to rise after a fall like I did.
Didn't get the chance to become all that he could've been.
But I carry that chance for him now.
I carry his name into every room I walk into.

His story didn't end the day his life was taken.
It lives on through the love we still have for him.
Through the way we speak his name.
Through the way we fight for young men like him—boys who feel invisible, discarded, caught in the crossfire of a world that doesn't always value their lives.

I still feel that loss like a weight some days.

It hits me in the quiet moments, in the memories that sneak up on me, in the milestones he'll never reach.

But I've learned to let that pain become purpose.

To speak louder.

To love harder.

To show up for the next generation like I wish someone could've for him.

Because his life mattered too.

And no matter how loud the world gets,

my voice will be louder—for both of them.

For every young soul who never got the chance to grow old.

For every boy who didn't make it out but left behind a story that still needs to be told.

And maybe the most sacred part of all this?

Is that I've stopped wishing for the past to be different—and started thanking God that it led me here.

Because this peace I have now? It's paid for in scars. It's built on the backs of boys who never got the chance to grow into men. It's soaked in the prayers of broken-hearted mothers, sleepless nights, and second chances.

And I won't let it go to waste.

I'll use every breath to honor the ones who never got this far.

I'll write with their names on my heart.

I'll speak with their strength in my voice.

I'll walk forward knowing their lives added weight to my purpose— and fire to my calling.

And I carry these stories forward not just in memory, but in mission.

Because every step I take now is in honor of the ones who can't take theirs.

Every moment of peace I experience, I pray it multiplies to those still in the storm.

I'm no longer running from my past—I'm walking with it beside me, hand in hand with grace.
It no longer weighs me down—it lifts others up.

And I know deep in my bones that as long as I keep walking, keep sharing, keep showing up...
Then their voices will never be lost.

Their stories are not over.
Because I'm still here.
Still telling them.
Still living them out loud.
Still letting God use the ashes to grow something eternal.

And I'll keep carrying them into every opportunity God gives me.
Into every story I tell.
Into every young man I mentor who still doesn't see his worth.
Because their lives—cut short as they were—laid the path I now walk.

I am their echo.
I am their continuation.
I am the living proof that even in the wreckage, there's redemption.

And I've made peace with this truth:
Some of our healing won't come from forgetting what we lost,
but from remembering it fully—and still walking forward with love.

And then there's my mama.

My solid rock.
My silent warrior.
The woman whose love I often took for granted, but whose presence held me together more times than I can count.

She's the one who answered the phone when I was locked up.
Who cried more tears in prayer than I ever did in pain.
She carried hope for me when I had none left for myself.

Looking back now, I can see it clear—
I didn't just survive because of a program or a pastor or a counselor.
I survived because my mother never stopped believing that God wasn't finished with me yet.

I know I put her through hell.
The sleepless nights. The missed birthdays. The unanswered calls. The lies.
The fear that would grip her heart when she hadn't heard from me and didn't know if I was alive.
But she never gave up. Never stopped praying.
Never stopped loving me, even when I was hard to love.

At this stage in my life, I realize something I never used to say out loud:
I wouldn't be the man I am today without her.

Her strength, her loyalty, her quiet faith—they laid a foundation I'm just now learning how to stand on.
She's the kind of mother whose prayers reach places even my words never could.
She held on when I let go.
She fought in the spirit when I was too tired to fight at all.

Mama, if you're reading this—I love you more than words can say.
You weren't just a part of my story.
You held it together when everything else was falling apart.
You've taught me more about unconditional love than any sermon ever could.

Thank you for being my anchor, even in the storms I created.
Thank you for seeing the man I could become, even when I couldn't see it myself.

And thank you for being the kind of woman I now hope my future daughter-in-law will be.

You are, and will always be, one of God's greatest gifts to me.

And I pray I make you proud—not just in words, but in the way I live what you helped save.

💬 Reflection Prompt:
Are there names, moments, or memories you've been afraid to speak out loud?

What would it look like to turn that pain into purpose, that grief into legacy?

Write it out. Give it a voice. Let the silence end with you.

📖 Scripture:
Psalm 34:18 (KJV)
The Lord is nigh unto them that are of a broken heart; and saveth such as be of a contrite spirit.

Chapter Nineteen

If you want to know who I am—
Don't just ask me what I've overcome.
Look at what I've become.
Because this life I live now?
It's not polished.
It's not perfect.
But it's powerful—because it's real.
I don't need a platform to prove it.
I don't need a spotlight or a stage.
I am the evidence.
My peace is the proof.
My son still calling me is the proof.
My clean hands, my clear mind, my daily surrender—that's the proof.

There was a time I thought my story would end in silence.
Buried under another relapse, another mugshot, another headline
nobody cared to read.

But now I realize—God never wanted to erase my story.
He just wanted to rewrite the ending.
And brother, He's still writing.

Every moment I breathe now feels like a miracle.
Not because it's flashy or dramatic—but because it's free.
I'm free to love.
Free to show up.
Free to feel everything I once ran from.
Free to laugh without guilt.
Free to cry without shame.
Free to live without wondering if I deserve to.

I do.
Not because I earned it—
But because Jesus paid for it.
I walk into rooms now that I once would've avoided.
I answer calls I used to let ring.
I say "yes" to things that would've terrified me.
And not because I've figured it all out—
But because I've finally realized: This life is worth showing up for.

There's power in presence.
There's healing in honesty.
And there's fire in just being who God called you to be.
Not the cleaned-up version.
Not the fake-it-till-you-make-it one.
But the raw, redeemed, battle-tested, grace-covered, chain-snapping real you.

I've been the addict.
I've been the absentee father.
I've been the ashamed nephew.
I've been the lost cause.
I've been the prisoner of my own choices.

I've been the one lying awake at night, wondering if the cycle would ever break.
I've stared into the mirror and not recognized the man looking back at me.
I've wept in motel bathrooms with bloodshot eyes, thinking there's no way out.
I've held the weight of a thousand regrets and tried to bury them in smoke.
I've missed moments I'll never get back.
I've hurt people who loved me.
I've broken promises that still echo in the hearts of those I made them to.

But by the grace of God—

Now I'm the man who made it.

Now I'm the one who prays out loud.

The one who mentors men who remind me of who I was.

The one who stands in the gap for families who are praying their loved one will finally get it.

Now I'm the one people look to and say,
"If God can do that in him… maybe He can do it in me too."

I used to ask God, "Why didn't You stop me?"
Now I ask Him, "How can I be used?"
I don't just want to be a story that people read.
I want to be a door they walk through.
A path they can follow.
A hand they can hold while they're still in the fire.
Because I didn't just survive for myself—
I survived for others.

For the young man sitting in detox wondering if his life matters.

For the father on the floor begging for another chance.

For the mother praying her son makes it home this time.

For the ones who think they've gone too far, done too much, and stayed too lost.

I survived for the addict still chasing a numb that'll never be enough.

For the man stuck in the same cell I once sat in, wondering if anyone still believes in him.

For the son who just wants his dad to come home and mean it this time.

I survived for the men who sat next to me in chapel and couldn't find their voice.

For the ones who shook their heads and said, "Not me," while I kept saying, "Yes, you."

I survived for the ones who think God skipped over them, the ones too angry to pray, too hurt to hope.

Because I've been there too.

I am living proof that it's never too late.

Not for healing.
Not for hope.
Not for redemption.
Not for purpose.
Not for joy.

I'm not who I was.
I'm not even who I thought I'd be.
I'm exactly who God had in mind when He said,
"I will restore the years the locusts have eaten."

So, if you ask me who I am today?
I'm a man who's free.
A man who's present.
A man who prays for others like someone once prayed for me.
A man who's more than his past and dangerous to hell because I finally know my worth.
I am the temple He rebuilt.
I am the voice the enemy couldn't silence.
I am the son who came home.
I am the grandfather who will break every chain before it touches my grandson's shoulders.
This life I live?
It's the testimony.

I don't walk around with shame anymore—I walk around with fire.
Because if I can keep showing up, then someone else might finally believe they can too.

If I can keep living this out loud, then maybe one more son won't lose his father, one more mother won't bury her child, one more man won't believe the lie that he's too broken to be used.

That's what this is about now.
It's not about applause.
It's not about platforms.
It's not even about making up for the past.
It's about honoring the grace I've been given by giving it away.
Every conversation. Every prayer. Every moment of obedience.
I'm pouring it all out, because I know what it cost to be here.

I'll spend the rest of my life being a light in places I once stumbled through blind.
And if my story becomes a torch for someone else's path?
Then every scar, every stumble, every second in the valley—it was all worth it.

And I know I haven't come this far just to sit back and coast.
I didn't get free just to live a quiet life in the shadows.
I got free to fight.
To show up on the front lines of this spiritual war and remind the enemy that he lost when I got up off that floor and said, "Not today."

There's fire in me now that didn't come from hype—it came from healing.
It came from altar calls soaked in tears and long nights of doubt answered by whispers from God saying, "Keep going."

It came from brotherhood forged in brokenness, from Scripture that sliced through lies I'd lived by for decades.

I'm not perfect, but I'm planted.
I'm not spotless, but I'm surrendered.
And I'll take that kind of man over a polished mask any day.

So when people ask what recovery looks like—
I'll point to this life.
The one where I get to be fully present, fully used, and fully alive.

So when I stand before others—whether it's in a classroom, a chapel, a parking lot, or just across the dinner table—I speak with the weight of Heaven behind me.

Not because I've earned it.
But because I've endured.
Because I've been crushed and pressed and remade into something I never imagined I could be.

There's a confidence in me now that isn't loud—but it's unshakable.
It's built on nights when I should've died.
On prayers I whispered with my last ounce of strength.
On mornings I woke up and didn't want to live—but did anyway.

That's the kind of confidence no stage can give you.
It's the kind that comes from walking through fire… and walking out clean.

And I'm just getting started.
Because as long as I've got breath in my lungs and a pulse in this heart,
I'll keep building, keep serving, keep testifying.
Because if my story opens the door for even one soul to find freedom,
then I'll tell it a thousand more times.

I've also learned that healing doesn't mean forgetting—it means choosing to build anyway.

I still remember the dark days.
I still hear the echoes of the lies I once believed.
But now, when those voices try to come back, I don't run—I stand.
And I speak the truth over myself:
That I am forgiven.
That I am chosen.
That I am a son of the Most High God with a mission hell can't cancel.

There is legacy in my lungs now.

Every breath I take is a reminder that the story didn't end where the enemy thought it would.

Every heartbeat is another line in a song of redemption that only God could've written.

So, I'll keep walking this road—
Not just to celebrate where I've come from,
But to lead others to where they were always meant to go.

Because at the end of the day, when the crowds go home and the lights go off, it's not about the claps.
It's about the consistency.
It's about being the same man when no one is watching.
It's about calling your son just to say, "I love you."
About hugging your brother even when it's hard.
About praying for the ones who still talk about you like you haven't changed.

I've come to realize that true freedom shows up in how you treat people who don't clap for you.
It shows up when you show mercy instead of bitterness,
when you bless those who walked away,
when you answer hate with healing.

This isn't just a testimony—it's a responsibility.
To carry the light.
To leave the door open.
To go back for the ones who still think it's too late.

Because it's not.

There's one last truth I want to leave behind in this chapter of my life:
God didn't just save me from something—He saved me for something.
He rescued me from destruction not just to give me peace,
but to make me a peacemaker.
He restored my mind not just to clear the fog,

but to fill it with wisdom I could give away.

My past may be behind me, but my purpose is still in front of me.

And every day, I wake up and choose to chase that purpose down with everything I've got.
Not for applause.
Not for recognition.
But for the next man still caught in the cycle—
For the next family praying for a miracle—
For the little boy in a children's home who hasn't been rescued yet.

As long as I've got a voice,
I'll keep raising it.
As long as I've got a story,
I'll keep telling it.
As long as I've got a heart that beats,
I'll keep letting it burn for the ones who still believe they're too far gone.

Because no one is.
And I'll never stop living like that's true.

And maybe one day, when I'm old and gray, I'll sit on a porch swing with my grandson beside me, and he'll ask, "Papa, how did you make it through?"
And I'll look at him—not with pride, but with peace—and I'll say, "God never let go."

I'll tell him about the nights I didn't think I'd live, and the mornings I woke up surprised I still had breath.
I'll tell him about grace that outran my guilt.

About mercy that met me in motel rooms.
About Jesus showing up—not in stained glass buildings, but in the silence of surrender.

And I'll tell him, "Son, if you ever feel lost, remember—your bloodline carries redemption now."

Because the chains that tried to choke our legacy got snapped.
Because your Papa didn't just survive—he stood.

And now, it's your turn to run with the torch.

💬 Final Reflection Prompt:
What has God brought you through that you're now ready to speak boldly about?
Write out your own declaration.
Your own, "This is who I was... and this is who I am now."
Let your life preach before your lips ever do.

📖 Scripture:
Revelation 12:11 (KJV)
And they overcame him by the blood of the Lamb, and by the word of their testimony;
and they loved not their lives unto the death.

Chapter Twenty

When you walk through hell and live to tell the story,
you don't walk the same.
You don't talk the same.
You don't even breathe the same.
You carry weight—not as a burden, but as proof.
The scars don't just mark what hurt you.
They mark what healed.
They mark what survived.
They mark what God brought back to life.

And this story—my story—is no longer about what was lost.
It's about what's been reborn.

I used to be afraid of the light.
It exposed too much.
It asked too much.
It reminded me of everything I wasn't.
But now?
I run toward it.
Because I finally know that the light of God doesn't shame you.
It covers you.
It warms you.
It restores you.

That light doesn't burn—it builds.
It shines down on the broken places and says,
"This is where I'll begin again."

So here I am, standing in that light.
Not as a perfect man.

Not as a religious man.

But as a man who's been radically wrecked and rebuilt by the mercy of Jesus Christ.

There's no version of my life that makes sense without Him.

No scenario where I got clean, got free, found peace, and reclaimed my future without His hand on every page.

I've tasted what darkness offers.

I've slept in shame.

I've been the liar, the addict, the man who said, "This is just who I am."

But God said otherwise.

He said,

"You are my son. You are worth saving.

You are not too far gone.

And everything the enemy used to destroy you...

I will use to build a kingdom."

And He did.

These days, people ask me what keeps me going.

It's not motivation.

It's not adrenaline.

It's not even pride.

It's gratitude.

It's the way I still remember what it felt like to wake up in a stranger's house, high and empty.

It's the ache I still feel when I think about the years I wasn't there for my son.

It's the fire that burns every time I see someone going through what I barely survived.

I keep going because I got a second chance.

And I'm not about to waste it.

I live now with intention.

Every decision. Every word. Every breath.

I live to leave light behind.

I want people to feel hope when I walk in a room.
I want them to feel seen.
I want the addict to say, "If he made it out, maybe I can too."
I want my grandson to grow up in a world where the word "legacy"
doesn't mean shame—it means strength.
I want my son to look at me and say, "That's my dad. He came back."
I want God to look at me and say,
"You took the pain I allowed, and you gave it back to Me as purpose."

That's the full-circle moment.
It's not just about getting free.
It's about helping others find freedom too.
It's not just about being forgiven.
It's about forgiving yourself,
so you can walk without the weight.
It's not just about starting over.
It's about starting better.

And to the reader holding this book right now—
you might be wondering if your story can turn around too.
Let me say this as clearly as I can:
Yes. It can.
No matter how far you've fallen.
No matter how many relapses, how many broken promises, how many
scars you've hidden.

You are not too far.
You are not too damaged.
You are not too late.
God is still writing.
And He writes with grace, not guilt.

There's something powerful that happens when you finally believe you
were born for more.

You stop looking for escape routes…
and you start looking for assignments.

You stop praying to survive…
and you start praying to serve.
You stop asking, "Why me?"
and you start saying, "Send me."

This chapter isn't just the end of a book.
It's the start of a legacy.
Not because I'm anything special—
But because God is.
And He takes men like me—
the ones who almost gave up,
the ones who were written off,
the ones who broke their families and their own hearts—
and He breathes life into dry bones.
He says, "I can still use that."
And then He does.

So, what now?

Now, I stay faithful.
I stay honest.
I stay grounded in grace.
I keep showing up.
I keep telling the truth.
I keep holding the line for the man I used to be… and the men still out there who haven't come home yet.
This is my call.
This is my offering.
This is my life.
A testimony in motion.
A flame that hell tried to extinguish.
A living, breathing reminder that Jesus still saves.
And that sometimes, the ones with the darkest pasts…
become the ones with the brightest future.

And let me tell you something I've learned along the way: it's not just about finishing the race—it's about how many people you carry with you while you're running.

It's about reaching back, stretching out your hand, and saying, "Come on, I've walked this path too."

It's about building more than a name. It's about building a bridge.
And that's what I want this story to be—
Not a monument to my survival, but a map for someone else's escape.

I want this chapter to echo in the ears of every man who thought he was done.
Every woman who believed the lies.
Every teenager trapped in silence, wondering if they'll ever feel whole again.
I want them to feel a shaking in their soul when they read these words:
You can come home.
You can begin again.
You can be restored.

Because I did.
And by the grace of God,
I still am.

And as I move forward, I know I'm not just walking for me anymore.
I'm walking for every man who's still locked up in a cell—whether it's a prison or his own mind.

I'm walking for every brokenhearted mother praying for her son to come home.
I'm walking for every father who thinks it's too late to be a good one.
I'm walking for every soul who's still drowning in secrets, still hiding their wounds.

And I want them to know:
You are not forgotten.
You are not disqualified.

You are not defined by your lowest moment.
You are seen. You are loved. You are still called.

The same God who met me in motel rooms, jail cells, and courtroom benches…

He's still showing up.
Still calling.
Still healing.
Still redeeming.

And if you're still breathing, there's still time.
There's still hope.
There's still a purpose with your name on it.
So don't give up.
Lean in. Hold on.
Let Him finish what He started in you.

And here's what I believe with every fiber of my being:
this story—this long, messy, grace-soaked, miracle-filled story—was never just for me.

It was for the sons still hoping their dad will get it right.
For the daughters wondering if healing will ever touch their family.
For the men in the back row who think they've disqualified themselves from redemption.

God let me survive what I did not just so I could tell it,
but so I could live it in front of others who are still in the struggle.
Not just talk about victory—but walk in it daily, honestly, and with humility.

Because somebody out there doesn't need a perfect preacher.
They need a wounded warrior who still shows up.
Who still believes.
Who still falls to his knees and says, "Lord, thank You for not giving up on me."

So I'll keep running this race,
but I'll do it with my eyes wide open and my heart wide open too.
Because the only thing greater than being set free…
is helping someone else break their chains too.

And I don't just want this to be a chapter that ends with me.
I want it to start something in you.
Something that stirs.
Something that breaks loose in your chest and whispers, "There's more for you than this."
Because you weren't born to die in bondage.
You weren't created just to survive.
You were made to thrive. To rise. To shake the dust off your story and start building again.

This isn't just inspiration—it's an invitation.
Come see what God can do with nothing but a willing heart and a surrendered life.

I'm not smarter than you. I'm not stronger than you.
I just stopped running and started listening.
I started saying yes when everything in me said no.
And every yes to God became another brick in the road I'm now walking.

So if you've made it to this page—don't just close the book and move on.
Let it mark you.
Let it provoke a decision.
Let it launch a new beginning.

Because this story may be mine...
but the next chapter?

That could be yours.

💬 Final Reflection Prompt:

What story is God writing through your life right now?

What chapter are you in—and what would it look like to trust Him with the ending?

Close your eyes. Breathe deep. And speak this over yourself:

"I am not done. I am being written by the hand of God."

📖 Scripture:

Joel 2:25 (KJV)

And I will restore to you the years that the locust hath eaten...

A Closing Note from Me to You

If you made it this far, I want to say thank you—from the deepest part of me.

Thank you for walking through my story.

Thank you for not turning away when it got messy.

Thank you for letting my truth sit with you—raw, cracked, and honest.

This book wasn't written to impress anyone.

It was written because I lived through hell, and I couldn't keep quiet about how God brought me out.

Maybe you saw pieces of yourself in my past.

Maybe you're still in the storm.

Or maybe you've come through it and you're trying to figure out what to do with everything you've survived.

Wherever you are, hear me now:

You're not too far gone.

You're not beyond grace.

You're not invisible.

And you're definitely not alone.

I'm living proof that God can take a life that looks like a total loss and breathe purpose back into it.

Not overnight.

Not without pain.

But with power, mercy, and relentless love.
I'm not perfect. I never will be.

But I'm free.

And I'm here.

And now, so are you.

If this book lit a fire in you—don't let it go out.

Fan it. Feed it.

Use it to ignite someone else's.

And when the enemy whispers that you're still the same...

Remind him of what God already redeemed.

This isn't the end of your story.

It's just a plot twist

Epilogue

If you're still here… then I believe you're supposed to be.

I don't know what brought you to this book, or what battles you're facing right now.

But I want you to know this:

You matter.

You're not too far gone.

And the same God who rescued me… is reaching for you.

This story—my story—wasn't written to impress.

It was written to show you what grace looks like when it refuses to quit.

To remind you that even in your worst moments, you are still being pursued by love.

So, whether you're walking through addiction, rebuilding relationships, or just trying to figure out who you are...

Don't stop now.
Healing is real.

Peace is possible.

And purpose is already inside you—waiting to rise.

Final Prayer

Father God,

Thank You for the one reading this right now.

Thank You for keeping them alive through the nights they thought they wouldn't make it.

Thank You for every second chance You've given—seen and unseen.

I pray You would meet them where they are.
Wrap them in grace.

Break every chain still holding them back.
Heal the wounds they've buried.

And remind them they are loved, chosen, and called.
Give them courage to take the next step—whatever it looks like.

Let this book be a seed, not just a story.
And may their life become a testimony too.

In Jesus' name,

Amen.

John 15:16 (KJV)
Ye have not chosen me, but I have chosen you, and ordained you, that ye should go and bring forth fruit, and that your fruit should remain…

Discussion + Reflection Guide

Use this guide as a space to pause, process, and let your own story rise to the surface. You can go through it alone, with a mentor, in a recovery group, or with someone who's walking the same road.

◆ Chapters 1–4: The Roots of Brokenness
1. Which part of Brent's early story hit home for you the most—and why?
Journal your thoughts:

2. What parts of your past are you still trying to outrun or silence?
Journal your thoughts:

3. Have you ever believed you were too far gone for God to use? How has that shaped your choices?
Journal your thoughts:

◆ Chapters 5–8: The Battle Within
4. What "mask" have you worn in your life to hide pain? What would it take to take it off?
Journal your thoughts:

5. When was the moment you realized you needed help—or that God was reaching for you?
Journal your thoughts:

6. Brent talks about relapsing and returning—what keeps you coming back when you fall?
Journal your thoughts:

◆ Chapters 9–12: Turning Point and Restoration
7. Who has been your anchor in the storm—family, friends, mentors, God? Have you thanked them?
Journal your thoughts:

8. What kind of legacy do you want to leave behind? Are you living in a way that builds it?
Journal your thoughts:

9. Which chapter of your life are you still trying to heal from? What would healing look like there?
Journal your thoughts:

◆ Chapters 13–16: Purpose and Vision

10. How do you stay grounded in the day-to-day—not just surviving, but living with intention?
Journal your thoughts:

11. Where have you seen grace show up in your story, even when you didn't deserve it?
Journal your thoughts:

12. If you could speak to your past self like Brent did, what would you say?
Journal your thoughts:

◆ Chapters 17–20: Legacy and Launch
13. What doors do you believe God is opening for you now—and are you ready to walk through them?
Journal your thoughts:

14. What habits, relationships, or thought patterns still try to pull you back into old cycles?
Journal your thoughts:

15. After reading this book, what is God asking you to do next? Are you willing to say yes?
Journal your thoughts:

What Comes Next

Writing this book was a surrender.

But what's coming next?

That's the assignment.

This isn't the end of my story—it's the launch of a life that I've decided to live with purpose, obedience, and boldness.

I believe God is calling me to more than recovery...

He's calling me to reach people, disciple men, and speak life into the broken—because I know exactly what it feels like to be one.

In the coming seasons, I'll be:

📚 Writing more books—covering topics like relapse, rebuilding relationships, faith through recovery, fatherhood after addiction, and how to walk in purpose when you still feel unqualified.

🕐 Offering one-on-one coaching and mentorship—for those walking through addiction, fresh into recovery, or rebuilding their life from the ground up. I want to walk beside you, not just speak at you.

🔗 Speaking at churches, events, men's conferences, and recovery programs—anywhere God opens the door. I want to bring this testimony to the ones who need it most, because I know what a real story can do for a desperate soul.

If you'd like to connect about coaching or invite me to speak at your event, reach out and let's set it up.

Contact: soulrebirthdesigns@gmail.com
Social: @SoulReBirthDesigns
Digital Resources: Etsy.com/shop/SoulReBirthDesigns
Facebook: https://www.facebook.com/share/14GdAZvjyTj/

I don't have all the answers. I don't have a title or a seminary degree.

But what I do have is a fire that won't go out—and a story that God's still using to set others free.

I'm available. I'm willing. I'm ready.

Let's build the Kingdom. One story at a time.

— Brent

Let's Stay Connected

Hey friend,

If this book touched you, challenged you, or helped you take one step closer to healing—don't let that momentum stop here. I'd love to stay connected with you as you continue your journey.

Whether you want to share your story, ask for prayer, or just say what this book meant to you—I'm here.

You can reach me at:
📱 soulrebirthdesigns@gmail.com
📱 Follow on TikTok, Instagram, and Pinterest: @SoulReBirthDesigns
🛒 Check out my digital recovery tools, devotionals & journals:
⚪ Etsy.com/shop/SoulReBirthDesigns

I'm not a therapist, a pastor, or a polished speaker.

I'm just a man who made it out… and wants to help others do the same.

Let's walk this thing out together.

With love,

– Brent

Author. Survivor. Grandfather. Child of God.

About the Author

Brent is a survivor, storyteller, and servant walking in the freedom of God's grace. After more than two decades of addiction, pain, and self-destruction, Brent found hope and healing through Jesus Christ and the hard, holy road of recovery.

He is a graduate of the Teen Challenge program, currently serving as an intern while preparing to join staff at their brand-new center. Brent is also about to become a full-time student, continuing his journey of restoration by finishing what he once thought was lost.

Brent is a soon-to-be grandfather and the proud founder of Soul ReBirth Designs—an online store offering faith-based digital tools to help others walk in freedom, purpose, and healing.

His mission is simple: to tell the truth, love people hard, and show the world that God still writes comeback stories.

Brent lives by the words:

"I'm not who I used to be. I'm living proof that grace doesn't give up."

You can follow Brent's journey or connect with him at:

TikTok, Instagram, Pinterest: @SoulReBirthDesigns
Etsy.com/shop/SoulReBirthDesigns
Email: 19brentstewart81@gmail.com
Facebook: https://www.facebook.com/share/14GdAZvjyTj/